REPORT TO CONGRESS ON THE PERFORMANCE OF PORTS AND THE INTERMODAL SYSTEM

June 2005

U.S. DEPARTMENT OF TRANSPORTATION MARITIME ADMINISTRATION

This Page Intentionally Blank

Table of Contents

Executive Summary

The Congressional Request

The Conference Report to accompany the FY 2004 Omnibus Appropriations legislation[1] directs the Maritime Administration (MARAD) to report to the House and Senate Committees on Appropriations on the performance of the intermodal system with respect to the efficiency of the most congested ports. The conferees directed that:

> "… particular emphasis should be placed on summarizing the performance of the 14 strategic commercial ports during the military force build-up for Operation Iraqi Freedom and on identifying the most glaring deficiencies of the intermodal system as a whole. This report is to contain a thorough comparison of the most congested ports in terms of operational efficiency; identification of significant intermodal obstacles associated with each port; and a summary of future actions MARAD plans to take to address and improve the throughput of cargo in America's ports. The conferees expect MARAD to work with industry groups as well as the scientific community in the completion of this study."

In this report, MARAD provides an assessment of the conditions at commercial ports, and the movement of military cargo through the intermodal system during the Operation Iraqi Freedom (OIF) buildup. MARAD's assessment includes the performance of the major components of the intermodal system: waterside, port/terminal intermodal interface, and landside movements. Particular emphasis is given to the ability of the nation's commercial freight transportation infrastructure to handle an unexpected surge in cargo during a military deployment, such as OIF.

MARAD was unable to provide the requested comparison of the most congested ports in terms of operational efficiency due to a lack of consistent national port efficiency data. Given the diverse characteristics of U.S. ports, comparing port efficiency would require the creation of new methodologics and the collection of data that were not available for this report. To address this issue, MARAD developed an innovative approach to meet the Committees' request by collecting information directly via site visits and a limited number of structured interviews with stakeholders, rather than employing a traditional survey.

MARAD wishes to emphasize that while this report is presented by the agency, it is the product of close collaboration with other Department of Transportation (DOT) components, from the development of the data gathering framework to information analysis and presentation. This collaboration underscores how imperative it is to see transportation as a national intermodal system, not as separate unconnected parts. This report also reflects collaboration and input from the scientific community, the private sector, and state and local governments. It proceeds, above all, from an appreciation that our nation's transportation system must always rest on the essential foundation of a solid and sustained public/private-sector partnership.

---

[1] U.S. House of Representatives, Conference Committee on Appropriations, "Report 108-243, Departments of Transportation and Treasury and Independent Agencies Appropriations Bill, FY 2004" (Washington, DC, July 30, 2003), p. 132.

America's Intermodal Transportation System

America's "intermodal transportation system" combines numerous public and private transportation elements, all of which are essential to the nation's economy and defense. This Report discusses several areas where there are deficiencies or areas for improvement in this intermodal system, and touches briefly on some of the things that address these challenges. Ideally, the intermodal transportation system should operate much like a pipeline, moving goods seamlessly from supplier to customer. However, in today's world, choke points and interruptions in the flow of commerce are common. Robust intermodal connectivity is necessary to support the flow of global commerce and the deployment of military forces. Only focused, sustained attention to the needs of both business and our military will allow for the creation of a truly seamless, integrated intermodal freight transportation system. Quite frankly, our country's economic future and security depends on it.

The principal components of our intermodal freight transportation infrastructure are:

- **The Marine Transportation System (MTS)**
- **Roads/Highways**
- **Railroads**
- **Pipelines**

In addition to the infrastructure, intermodal operations involve transportation professionals from a wide array of U.S. and world transportation interests, including truckers, freight forwarders, third-party logistics providers, waterfront labor, shipping agents, railroad engineers, terminal operators, marine vessel operators, commercial shippers, trade association representatives and numerous government agencies.

The MTS includes the inter-related components of the national transportation system, such as shipping, ports, inland waterways, and their connection to rail and highway transportation modes, and system users. The MTS is also more than a transportation system. It is a major employer in the United States and, through its expenditures for supplies and personnel, a major contributor to the nation's economy. All freight, on all modes of transportation, both domestic and international, moving in, out and within the United States in 2002 had a value of $9.1 trillion. Most of the international trade portion is waterborne and amounted to $2.0 trillion.[2]

Information Collection

During February 2004, information needed to assess intermodal efficiency and port performance was collected directly from key port, terminal, stevedore, and labor representatives at 23 ports by four MARAD-led DOT intermodal teams using a limited number of structured interviews. Discussions at the outreach sessions focused on the performance of major components of the intermodal system: waterside, port/terminal intermodal interface, and landside movements. Port-specific information was also gathered from other sources, including the Department of Defense (DOD), commercial shippers, and previous reports. The site visits included the ten commercial ports that participated in the early OIF deployment. The interview teams focused on two separate operating scenarios of the

---

[2] National Chamber Foundation, "Trade and Transportation: A Study of North American Port and Intermodal Systems", U.S. Chamber of Commerce, Washington, DC, 2003, p. 1.

MTS: normal commercial traffic, and the unique requirements of a military deployment through commercial ports. To ensure candid discussion, MARAD agreed to keep confidential the identities of those interviewed.

Port Performance During Operation Iraqi Freedom

MARAD found that during the early OIF deployment, the strategic commercial ports and the transportation industry were able to support the military requirements with minimal commercial cargo disruptions. Four of the ports – Jacksonville, FL, Beaumont, TX, Corpus Christi, TX and Charleston, SC – carried over 75 percent of the tonnage shipped from the continental United States ports. The occasional congestion problem was resolved within a few days. The impact of a deployment can vary by port and situation; however, there was greater urgency in the four ports that moved most of the volume.

OIF has provided the U.S. Government with a unique opportunity to "stress test" our strategic commercial ports and mobilization technologies. The strategic commercial ports and the transportation industry did an outstanding job of supporting the military in OIF with minimal commercial cargo disruptions. However, a number of impediments were identified that need to be addressed so future deployments can work equally well, particularly as the transportation system becomes more congested in the years ahead.

Intermodal System Challenges

The MTS' greatest challenge is the projected growth in our international trade, and the ability of the marine, highway and rail systems to accommodate the increased volumes of freight shipments so vital to our nation's continued economic growth. DOT now projects that total freight volumes will increase by more than 50 percent in the next 20 years. While domestic waterborne trade is expected to grow modestly, U.S. international container traffic is projected to at least double from 2001 to 2020. Nowhere will this pressure be felt more than at U.S. ports. As trade volumes increase, the capacity of America's total intermodal transportation system must increase in order to maintain and expand the nation's economy.

Military operational deployments require the large-scale use of Roll-on/Roll-off (RO/RO) ships, which are capable of carrying a combination of aircraft, wheeled and tracked vehicles, oversize equipment, and containers. As demonstrated during OIF, loading of combat units requires substantial staging areas for vehicles and aircraft, adequate port rail infrastructure, and port labor that is skilled in handling non-containerized military equipment. Therefore, the effectiveness of military cargo operations at the ports is directly tied to the mobility planning process and the availability of staging areas and rail infrastructure for sequencing such equipment arriving from the military installations. U.S. ports will continue to expand their operations to meet the forecasted growth in commercial containerized freight. If ports reduce the area available for non-containerized cargo, facilities needed to support the unique military cargo handling requirements will become scarcer and this may reduce the ability of U.S. ports to facilitate future military unit deployments.

Security is a new major challenge for the intermodal system. The goal of both industry and the government is to protect the nation against the catastrophic impact of a terrorist act and at the same time not hamper the flow of trade, which would disrupt the nation's economy. The new security imperative will be an everyday challenge for transportation providers, especially ports, in terms of operations and resources until security is integrated into everyday operations.

Port Intermodal Obstacles

The greatest concerns for both commercial operations and military deployments were the surge in cargo flows into the ports, the adequacy of cargo staging areas in the ports, port rail infrastructure, and communications. Additional issues that dominated commercial operations were landside access to ports, highway signage, channel and port dredging, increasing cargo volumes, financing, and intermodal connectivity. Two additional major concerns specific to military deployments were training and coordination among ports and shippers.

While there were a wide variety of themes in response to MARAD's questions, there was much agreement on the most urgent congestion and infrastructure issues facing the MTS. About half the ports cited specific reasons for congestion that cause infrastructure overload. One fourth of the ports described their infrastructure impediments as "severe." The responses mirror the concerns raised in recent DOT, Government Accountability Office (GAO), and non-government studies on MTS issues.

Conclusion

Operation Iraqi Freedom's test of the Nation's mobilization capacity highlights the fact that our transportation system must operate in an integrated, intermodal manner if we are to respond quickly to future mobilizations. In addition to the growing volume of cargo moving through our Nation's ports and the increased security challenges throughout the MTS, there are 17 Federal agencies in six cabinet-level departments currently responsible for maritime decision-making. In the past, this has led to a patchwork of inefficient laws, polices, and programs.

That is why President Bush, in his response to the Commission on Oceans Policy, has called for the Department of Transportation to work with other Federal agencies with responsibilities associated with the MTS to improve interagency coordination. This will be accomplished by elevating the existing Interagency Committee on the Marine Transportation System (ICMTS) to the cabinet level and using that forum to assess MTS needs, review Federal and non-Federal programs designed to meet those needs, and identify ways to fill any remaining gaps. The result will be a more integrated MTS policy-making structure across the Federal government, which will help us to ensure that we can continue to support our troops when called upon to do so.

Previous reports and studies also point to a need for system-wide investments in the national transportation system with better coordination of expenditures on highways, public mass transit, rail, airports, MTS, and other essential intermodal connectors where they intersect. As DOT/ MARAD move to take a more systemic approach to MTS policy development, by better integrating the public and private sectors, as well as local, State, and Federal interests, we must do so as part of a coordinated national transportation policy across all modes. With this approach, we can also identify the intermodal infrastructure investment and public and private partnerships needed to build an integrated freight system that can meet future commercial and national defense requirements.

Despite progress in the 1991 Intermodal Surface Transportation Efficiency Act (ISTEA) and the Transportation Equity Act for the 21st Century (TEA-21) to improve intermodal connectivity, significant gaps still exist in programs, policies, and funding related to creating and maintaining an intermodal system which functions as the kind of seamless system we need to compete in the global economy. In response, the Administration has proposed a series of freight related initiatives in the Safe, Accountable, Flexible, and Efficient Transportation Equity Act of 2003 (SAFETEA). These include dedicated funding for intermodal connectors between major highways and ports or rail facilities, up to $15 billion in private activity bonds to fund highway and intermodal projects, and the creation of a freight coordinator in each state to ensure that freight-related projects get sufficient attention in state and regional planning processes.

Given current needs and projected requirements that will be placed on America's national transportation system and its essential marine mode component, DOT/ MARAD believe that comprehensive marine transportation system improvements, which include the full integration of a strengthened marine mode into the national intermodal system, are essential. At the direction of the President, the Administration is exploring ways of strengthening Federal Government coordination and management of the Marine Transportation/Maritime Industry.

This targeted approach is expected to include strengthening Federal Government coordination and management, conducting a thorough assessment of MTS needs across the system, and the removal of non-market obstacles that impede development of U.S. maritime industries. As part of this effort, DOT/ MARAD will also focus on leveraging funds from Federal, state and local governments, as well as the private sector, to address MTS needs and ensure broad state and local government and private sector input. The ultimate goal is to deliver a marine transportation system that enhances the efficiency, productivity, and capacity of our nation's intermodal transportation system. The better utilization of America's waterways will mitigate the congestion that is otherwise inevitable as overland freight shipments increase.

Supplementing SAFETEA, which is now awaiting action by the Congress, the DOT/MARAD efforts will help meet the challenges of the future; especially much needed infrastructure repair and replacement. Progress toward the goal will require a sustained commitment from government and private sector leaders alike. In addition, the successful implementation of these much-needed improvements will generate significant economic activity, increase tax revenues, and create American jobs, both while these projects are underway and well into the future.

This Page Intentionally Blank

Chapter I. Ports and the Intermodal System

A. Congressional Request

The Conference Report to accompany the FY 2004 Omnibus Appropriations legislation[3] directs the Maritime Administration (MARAD) to report to the House and Senate Committees on Appropriations on the performance of the intermodal system with respect to the efficiency of the most congested ports. The conferees directed that:

> "… particular emphasis should be placed on summarizing the performance of the 14 strategic commercial ports during the military force build-up for Operation Iraqi Freedom and on identifying the most glaring deficiencies of the intermodal system as a whole. This report is to contain a thorough comparison of the most congested ports in terms of operational efficiency; identification of significant intermodal obstacles associated with each port; and a summary of future actions MARAD plans to take to address and improve the throughput of cargo in America's ports. The conferees expect MARAD to work with industry groups as well as the scientific community in the completion of this study."

The Committees' request provides an opportunity for MARAD to report on the current performance of the nation's intermodal system as a whole. For this report, MARAD interpreted the Committees' request as follows:

- Summarize the performance of the 14 strategic commercial ports during the military force build-up for Operation Iraqi Freedom (OIF) (Chapters I and III);

- Compare the most congested ports in terms of operational efficiency, using available information sources (Chapters I and II);

- Identify the most glaring deficiencies of the intermodal system as a whole as they relate to ports (Chapters II and III);

- Identify significant intermodal obstacles associated with each port (Chapter III, identified system-wide rather than port-specific); and

- Summarize future actions MARAD plans to take to address and improve the throughput of cargo in America's ports (Chapter V).

B. Description of America's Intermodal Transportation System

America's "intermodal transportation system" combines numerous public and private transportation elements, all of which are essential to the nation's economy and defense. While America's transportation system is robust and performing well, it has yet to become a seamless, integrated intermodal freight transportation system. In addition to its infrastructure, the system includes

---

[3] U.S. House of Representatives, Conference Committee on Appropriations, "Report 108-243, Departments of Transportation and Treasury and Independent Agencies Appropriations Bill, FY 2004" (Washington, DC, July 30, 2003), p. 132.

transportation professionals from a wide array of U.S. and world transportation interests, including truckers, freight forwarders, third party logistics providers, waterfront labor, shipping agents, railroad engineers, terminal operators, marine vessel personnel, marine vessel operators, and trade association representatives. The principal system components of our nation's intermodal transportation infrastructure are:

1. **The Marine Transportation System (MTS):** The MTS includes the interrelated components of the national transportation system, such as shipping, ports, inland waterways, and their connection to rail and highway transportation modes, and system users. The MTS is also more than a transportation system. It is a major domestic employer and, through its expenditures for supplies and personnel, a major contributor as an industry to the nation's economy. The MTS includes over 361 public and private deepwater and intercoastal waterway ports and over 24,000 miles of inland and coastal navigable waterways. The Department of Defense (DOD) relies on the MTS commercial system for moving cargo through ports in peacetime and during mobilization. The National Port Readiness Network (NPRN) and the 14 Strategic Ports provide direct support to DOD.[4] A detailed description of the NPRN is provided in Appendix A.

2. **Roads/Highways:** The National Highway System (NHS) consists of approximately 160,000 miles of Federal, State, and local roadways, including the Eisenhower Interstate System and the Strategic Highway Network (STRAHNET). This network of highways is important to the United States' strategic defense policy and provides access, continuity, and emergency response capabilities. Also important to DOD are the various state and local intermodal connector roads that allow for efficient transfers of cargo between different transportation modes.

3. **Rail:** The nation's rail system consists of a private rail network with 174,000 miles of track connecting all 48 contiguous states, as well as Canada and Mexico. Through an agreement between the Departments of Defense and Transportation, the railroads have in place a Strategic Rail Corridor Network (STRACNET). STRACNET is the designation given to those civilian rail lines (a 30,000 mile interconnected network plus connectors to military installations) that are most important to national defense.

4. **Pipelines**: The U.S. pipeline system consists of 2.1 million miles of oil and natural gas pipelines. Pipelines deliver at very low cost the crude oil that refineries convert into essential materials for core American industries, such as plastics, pharmaceuticals and agriculture, as well as gasoline. Pipelines are the safest and least expensive method of delivering energy necessary to meet the growing demand for military and consumer needs.

Ideally, the intermodal transportation system should operate much like a pipeline, moving goods seamlessly from supplier to customer. However, in today's world, choke points and interruptions in the flow of commerce are common. Robust intermodal connectivity is necessary to support the flow

---

[4] The strategic ports used in early OIF were Jacksonville, FL, Beaumont, TX, Corpus Christi, TX, Charleston, SC, San Diego, CA,, Morehead City, NC , Wilmington, NC, Savannah, GA, Tacoma, WA and Norfolk/Newport News, VA. The other five strategic ports are New York/New Jersey, Philadelphia, PA, Morehead City, NC, Long Beach, CA, and Oakland, CA. Although the strategic commercial ports have been specifically designated by DOD and MARAD to support major force deployments and military force build-up under one or more of our national defense contingency plans, DOD is not restricted to using only these ports.

of global commerce and the deployment of military forces. The transportation system must strike a balance for all of its components such that none are undersized or inefficient, thereby causing a "bottleneck" in the port itself or in connecting rail and highway access lines to a port. The term "connectivity" refers to a ports' need to have efficient waterside and landside connections (highway and rail access) as shown in Figure 1.

Figure 1

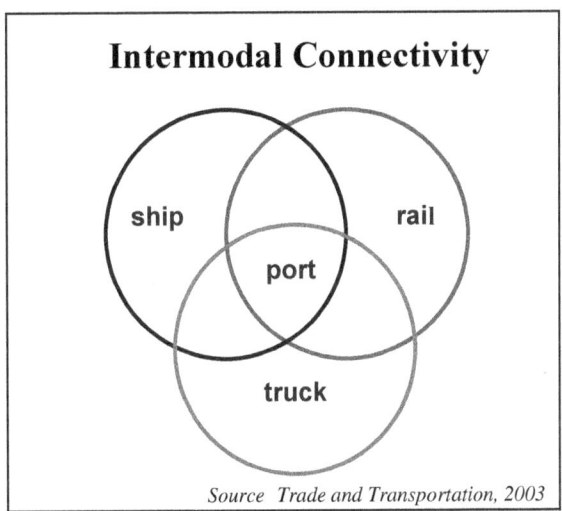

Source Trade and Transportation, 2003

Major forces having an impact on conditions in our intermodal system include the growth in international trade, and the ability of the marine, highway and rail systems to accommodate the increased volumes of freight shipments so vital to our nation's continued economic growth. All freight, on all modes of transportation, both domestic and international, moving in, out and within the United States in 2002 had a value of $9.1 trillion.[5]

Most of the international trade portion is waterborne and amounted to $2.0 trillion and represents nearly 20 percent of annual world waterborne trade. Containerized manufactured goods moving through our ports are the fastest growing segment of international trade, accounting for $700 billion. As the Government Accountability Office, formerly the General Accounting Office (GAO), recognized: "Because more than 95 percent of our nation's overseas trade tonnage moves by water, container ports are key gateways for our nation's imports and exports and, therefore, play a particularly critical role in moving goods into and across the country. Increasing congestion at these seaports and the surrounding metropolitan areas is a growing national concern and represents a threat to the efficient flow of the nation's goods."[6] Canada and Mexico are not included in overseas trade, since U.S. trade with these countries is primarily over land.

---

[5] National Chamber Foundation, "Trade and Transportation: A Study of North American Port and Intermodal Systems", U.S. Chamber of Commerce, Washington, DC, 2003, p. 1.

[6] Government Accountability Office, formerly the General Accounting Office (GAO), "Freight Transportation: Strategies Needed to Address Planning and Financing Limitations, GAO-04-165" (Washington, DC, December 2003), p. 1.

C. Focus of this Report on Selected Commercial Ports

In this report, MARAD provides an assessment of the conditions at commercial ports, and the movement of military cargo through the intermodal system during the OIF buildup. MARAD's assessment includes the performance of the major components of the intermodal system: waterside, port/terminal intermodal interface, and landside movements. Particular emphasis is given to the ability of the nation's commercial freight transportation infrastructure to handle an unexpected surge in cargo during a military deployment such as OIF.

For this report, MARAD assessed the conditions at U.S. ports and the intermodal system from three key inter-connected perspectives, as shown in Figure 2:

- conditions existing at the ten strategic ports used during the OIF deployment;

- commercial conditions generally at all 14 strategic ports and the other ports that are ranked as the top 20 continental U.S. containerized ports; and

- an overview for conditions in U.S. ports and their intermodal connectors system-wide.

Figure 2

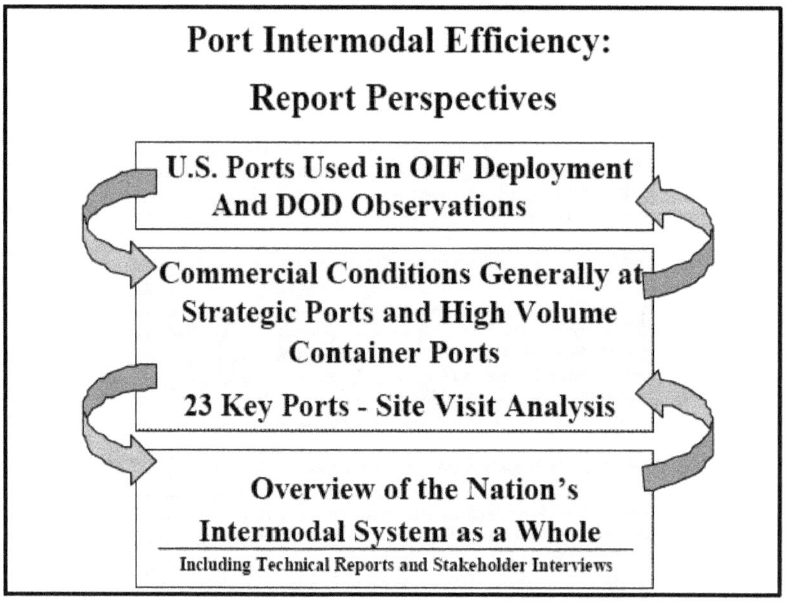

Port Intermodal Efficiency:

Report Perspectives

U.S. Ports Used in OIF Deployment And DOD Observations

Commercial Conditions Generally at Strategic Ports and High Volume Container Ports

23 Key Ports - Site Visit Analysis

Overview of the Nation's Intermodal System as a Whole

Including Technical Reports and Stakeholder Interviews

1. Ports Included in this Report

For this report, MARAD focused particularly on the ten strategic commercial ports used in the early OIF deployment. MARAD also analyzed in depth the other four strategic commercial ports that were not involved in the OIF deployment. To complement the assessment of conditions at the strategic ports, MARAD also included the other major container ports that are not strategic ports but are among the top 20 container ports in the continental United States (CONUS). This resulted in the 23 ports included in this report, as shown in Figure 3.

Figure 3

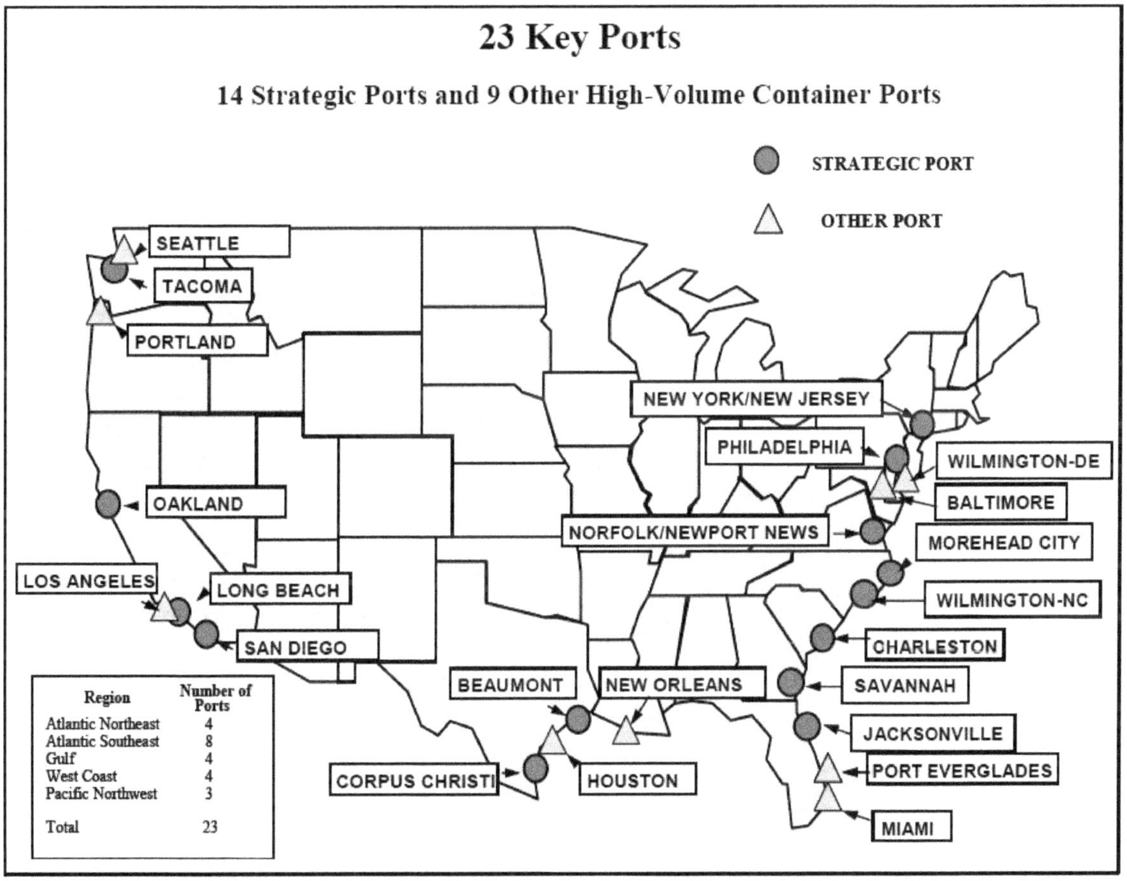

23 Key Ports

14 Strategic Ports and 9 Other High-Volume Container Ports

Region	Number of Ports
Atlantic Northeast	4
Atlantic Southeast	8
Gulf	4
West Coast	4
Pacific Northwest	3
Total	23

These 23 ports account for over 40 percent of the nation's international trade and domestic commerce. Total international and domestic freight handled through the 23 key ports is over one billion tons.[7] Table 1 shows the cargo volumes that passed through the 23 ports in 2002.

Table 1

Total Cargo Throughput for the 23 Selected Ports, 2002			
Ports	**Total Tonnage**	**General Cargo/Liner**	**TEUs**
Houston, (TX)	177,560,719	22,689,068	1,159,789
NY/NJ	**137,484,344**	**50,928,235**	**3,749,014**
New Orleans (LA)	85,628,353	36,206,785	302,318
Beaumont (TX)	**79,130,510**	**333,871**	**1,263**
Corpus Christi (TX)	**77,575,699**	**2,548,110**	**NA**
Long Beach (CA)	**67,643,920**	**35,630,408**	**4,524,038**
Los Angeles (CA)	51,395,952	48,084,750	6,110,001
Norfolk/Newport News (VA)	**51,170,320**	**39,742,114**	**1,437,779**
Philadelphia (PA)	**46,372,067**	**4,031,463**	**215,000**
Baltimore (MD)	42,072,123	6,110,001	508,000
Portland (OR)	31,339,470	2,808,386	255,745
Charleston (SC)	**23,250,058**	**10,595,803**	**1,592,834**
Port Everglades (FL)	21,915,409	4,446,138	554,041
Seattle (WA)	20,546,494	10,921,269	1,438,872
Tacoma (WA)	**20,523,372**	**11,383,839**	**1,470,826**
Savannah (GA)	**19,392,227**	**11,438,432**	**1,327,939**
Jacksonville (FL)	**17,809,488**	**6,986,933**	**683,836**
Oakland (CA)	**12,272,777**	**11,120,459**	**1,707,827**
Miami (FL)	8,513,909	7,639,257	981,000
Wilmington (DE)	6,419,677	4,134,230	244,564
Wilmington (NC)	**6,205,995**	**2,153,561**	**127,109**
Morehead City (NC)	**3,142,834**	**590,774**	**50,000**
San Diego (CA)	**3,120,555**	**2,076,100**	**13,188**
Total	**1,010,486,272**	**332,599,986**	**28,454,983**

Note: "Total Tonnage" is U.S. Army Corps of Engineers' data expressed in short tons, and includes all types of cargo and all handling modes, and illustrates the large volume of foreign and domestic tonnage having an impact on the transportation systems in and around the identified port. "General Cargo/Liner" freight excludes dry and liquid bulk cargoes and illustrates the large volume of general cargo flowing through the marine terminals. The column entitled "TEUs" (twenty-foot equivalent units) is the measure of containerized cargo. Strategic commercial ports are indicated in bold.

---

[7] Cargo volume data are maintained in different cargo measurements. In addition to TEUs and tons, general cargo shipments of wheeled and tracked vehicles are expressed in square feet. This report focuses on OIF cargo, which is expressed in square feet and tons. Wheeled and tracked vehicles, which comprised most of the OIF cargo, are very space intensive and create special pressures on the load-out ports.

2. Measuring Port Efficiency

In preparing this report, MARAD reviewed articles and studies from the academic and scientific communities that set forth methodologies for measuring port efficiency. The literature reviewed supported MARAD's finding that there is no widespread agreement on an approach to measuring the efficiency of a port as a link in the logistics chain. A 2004 article in *Maritime Policy & Management* states: "Measures of port efficiency or performance indicators use a diverse range of techniques for assessment and analysis, but although many analytical tools and instruments exist, a problem arises when one tries to apply them to a range of ports and terminals. Ports are very dissimilar and even within a single port the current or potential activities can be broad in scope and nature, so that the choice of an appropriate tool of analysis is difficult. Organizational dissimilarity constitutes a serious limitation to enquiry, not only concerning what to measure but also how to measure. Furthermore, the concept of efficiency is vague and proves difficult to apply in a typical port organization extending across production, trading and service industries."[8]

There are many factors to be considered in assessing port performance. A few examples of factors that affect port throughput and performance are summarized below.

Factors that Affect Port Cargo Volume:

- Type of cargoes handled by the port (specialization)
- Location of port relative to shippers' markets (regional demand)
- Price of port services relative to shippers' alternative ports
- Waterside access limitations
- Carrier investment in port infrastructure
- Quality of port services
- Business realignment to increase purchasing power
- Availability of national government subsidies

Factors that Affect Port Efficiency:

- Labor efficiency (cargo moved per unit of labor)
- Land use efficiency (cargo storage per unit of land)
- Waterside access limitations
- Capacity of port road and rail connections
- Inland transportation availability
- Cargo handling capability

The diversity of these factors, and the lack of uniform data collection, prevents the general measurement of port efficiency. As noted in a recent paper presented at the International Association of Maritime Economists:

---

[8] Khalid Bichou and Richard Gray, "A Logistics and Supply Chain Management Approach to Port Performance Measurement," Maritime Policy & Management, Vol. 31, No. 1, January–March 2004, pp. 47–67.

"Despite the importance of port performance measurement, however, it is surprising to note that there are almost no standard methods that are accepted as applicable to every port for the measurement of its performance (Cullinane, 2002). More surprisingly, it is even harder to find standard terminology to describe port production, with different container ports using different terms to describe port production. '*Measurement will always have a natural tendency to be terminal-specific*' (Robinson, 1999). As reported by De Monie (1987), the measurement of port productivity has been greatly impeded by the following factors:

- The sheer number of parameters involved;
- The lack of up-to-date, factual and reliable data, collected in an accepted manner and available for dissemination;
- The absence of generally agreed and acceptable definitions;
- The profound influence of local factors on the data obtained; and
- The divergent interpretation given by various interests to identical results"[9]

MARAD concluded that it was unable to provide the requested comparison of the most congested ports in terms of operational efficiency due to a lack of consistent national port efficiency data. Given the diverse characteristics of U.S. ports, comparing port efficiency would require the creation of new methodologies and the collection of data that were not available for this report. To address this issue, MARAD developed an innovative approach to meet the Committees' request by collecting information directly via site visits and a limited number of structured interviews with stakeholders, rather than employing a traditional survey. The methodology is further explained and the results are presented in detail in Chapter II.

D. Summary of the Performance of the Strategic Ports During Operation Iraqi Freedom

The results of MARAD's analysis show that OIF cargo was able to move through the strategic ports simultaneously with commercial freight, with a few exceptions. Congestion related to the OIF surge only lasted a short time and the occasional congestion problem was resolved within a few days. However, this performance should not suggest complacency regarding preparedness for future military deployments through U.S. ports. The projected growth of domestic commerce and international trade must be met with a corresponding growth in freight capacity lest future urgent deployments result in costly disruption of commerce and delays in logistics support for such deployments.

The following table (Table 2) with information provided by SDDC, shows that during the OIF force buildup from January 13 to May 23, 2003, nine strategic commercial ports managed nearly 70 percent of the over 1.1 million tons (21 million square feet) of OIF cargo shipped from foreign and

---

[9] Wang, T-F, Song, D-W, and Cullinane, K. P. B., "The Applicability of Data Envelopment Analysis to Efficiency Measurement of Container Ports," presented at the International Association of Maritime Economists, Panama Conference, November 2002, p. 6.

domestic ports[10]. Of the total amount shown, nearly half was carried in the first two months. Four of the ports – Jacksonville, FL, Beaumont, TX, Corpus Christi, TX and Charleston, SC – carried over 75 percent of the tonnage shipped from the CONUS ports. In addition to the strategic commercial ports, other U.S. and foreign ports were used as part of the force build-up.

Table 2

OIF Cargo Moved January-May 2003*				
			Percent of Total Tonnage	
Strategic Ports	**Square Footage**	**Tonnage**	**From All Ports**	**From U.S. Ports Only**
Jacksonville (FL)	3,622,457	148,147	13.41%	16.31%
Beaumont (TX)	3,326,773	170,075	15.39%	18.72%
Corpus Christi (TX)	2,936,800	144,624	13.09%	15.92%
Charleston (SC)	2,648,325	118,208	10.70%	13.01%
San Diego (CA)	866,310	47,837	4.33%	5.27%
Wilmington (NC)	826,105	50,232	4.55%	5.53%
Savannah (GA)	686,402	27,355	2.48%	3.01%
Tacoma (WA)	135,483	6,299	0.57%	0.69%
Norfolk/Newport News (VA)	28,000	56,598	5.12%	6.23%
Total Strategic Ports	15,076,655	769,375	69.63%	84.70%
Total Other U.S. Ports	2,198,906	138,932	12.57%	15.30%
Total All U.S. Ports	17,275,561	908,307	82.20%	100.00%
Total Foreign Ports	3,862,517	196,668	17.80%	
Grand Total All Ports	21,138,078	1,104,975	100.00%	
*Note: Cargo volume data is maintained in different cargo measurements. For this report, containerized cargo is expressed in TEUs and/or tons. Other general cargo is expressed in tons or square feet for wheeled or tracked vehicles. Liquid cargo is expressed in tons.				
Source: USTRANSCOM: Strategy, Plans, Policy and Programs Directorate				

DOD, through MARAD, worked with the NPRN Steering Group, Working Group and Port Readiness Committees to coordinate final planning for the OIF deployment. (Explanation of these committees is in Appendix A) The high level of cooperation between military and commercial interests to support the OIF effort kept disruptions to a minimum throughout the deployment. Because OIF cargo was able to move through the ports with only minor delays, DOT intervention to establish priority use of strategic ports and to issue National Shipping Authority Service Priority Orders were not necessary for this deployment.[11]

---

[10] The Marines self-deployed from Morehead City, NC i.e. the volume of cargo that they shipped is not reported to SDCC and is not included in the above table.

[11] Pursuant to the Defense Production Act of 1950 (DPA), DOD can request that DOT require strategic commercial ports to provide priority use of their facilities and services to DOD ahead of their normal commercial contractual obligations.

A military deployment such as OIF tests the ability of the nation's commercial freight transportation infrastructure to handle an unexpected surge in cargo. Our national defense strategy calls for rapid deployment and sustainment of massive combat power, utilizing a combination of government-owned and commercial sealift assets. International conflicts necessitate mobilization by sea, a cornerstone of our mobilization strategy. To meet its sealift deployment requirements, DOD uses its surge sealift fleet composed of Large Medium Speed Roll-on/Roll-off Ships (LMSRs), Fast Sealift Ships (FSSs), Maritime Prepositioning Ships (MPSs), and ships in MARAD's Ready Reserve Force (RRF), as well as commercial vessels for shipments of sustainment cargo. These vessels are capable of carrying a combination of aircraft, wheeled and tracked vehicles, oversize equipment, and containers.

The logistical backbone for deployment of American forces and materiel, from the "fort to foxhole," relies on the commercial intermodal freight transportation system. This vital military cargo is overlaid on the transportation system, which is already stressed by carrying commercial freight with demanding delivery schedules.

Virtually all CONUS based military contingency cargoes are deployed through U.S. commercial seaports, with the exception of ammunition and other specialized or dangerous cargoes. Whereas commercial cargo and peacetime military cargo are primarily containerized, OIF military cargo is based on moving an entire military unit's needs (force package) and contains wheeled vehicles, tanks, and other materiel. Military surge and sustainment freight also differs in volume and needed configuration. This surge deployment of OIF cargo puts unique pressure on staging areas and requires the use of other labor skills to load the cargo.

Military freight for a mobilization moves under compressed timeframes, with a requirement to maintain real-time communications between public and private transportation entities and DOD command and control. As a result, military operations, if not properly planned, coordinated and executed, can be disruptive to commercial transportation operations both immediately and over the longer-term. For example, U.S.-based forts may load and dispatch six trains per-day to ports, while the receiving port may only have the capability of handling and unloading one to two trains per day. Military deployments, which must preserve unit integrity, may require that a port receive materials and supplies from more than a dozen different U.S. military installations in a short timeframe. Trains and trucks may be dispatched from bases and arrive at the terminal gates with little advance warning. DOD logistics planners have adopted successful commercial methods of handling freight and will re-direct cargo at the last moment to accomplish a just-in-time (JIT) delivery. Usually these changes occur with little or no warning to the receiving port.

To make better use of the commercial transportation system, DOD is rapidly changing its focus from traffic management, which reacts to uncoordinated inputs from the supply-side, to a distribution-based organization that focuses on seamless end-to-end processes. In 2002, the U.S. military was ranked 30th on the Journal of Commerce list of "Top 100 Containerized Exporters." Because the military has become a commercial user of the ports' infrastructure during peacetime, military deployments during a crisis will be able to flow more efficiently through the nation's freight system along with commercial cargo causing only minimal delays.

E. Multiple Challenges Facing the Intermodal System

1. Projected Growth in Trade

The projected growth in international trade, and the ability of the marine, highway, and rail systems to accommodate the increased volumes of freight shipments so vital to continued economic growth, will have an impact on the ability of our nation's intermodal system to perform efficiently. The U.S. intermodal transportation system (all land, water, and air modes) annually moves more than 15 billion tons of freight, with a total value of over $9.1 trillion.[12] DOT now projects that total freight volumes will increase by more than 50 percent in the next 20 years. As trade volumes increase, the capacity of America's total intermodal transportation system must also increase in order to maintain and expand our nation's economy.

The MTS consists of inland waterways, ports, intermodal connectors, vessels, vehicles, and system users. Growth in trade resulting from market globalization has been, and continues to be, the greatest challenge facing the MTS, and reinforces the need for a truly systemic approach to multi-modal national freight transportation. Global markets will continue to drive increases in imports and exports. Industries will continue to redefine themselves; new industries will emerge, and old ones will fade. The dynamic character of supply chain innovations and security needs will continue to place pressure on the transportation system. While domestic waterborne trade is expected to grow modestly, U.S. international container traffic is projected to at least double from 2001 to 2020. Nowhere will this pressure be felt more than at U.S. ports, which serve as gateways for both military and commercial cargo.

Since the advent of containerization in the early 1960's, ports have had to keep up with significant evolving changes in vessel and shoreside infrastructure needs. Container vessel capacities have grown from 500+ TEU ships to over 8,000 TEUs, and next generation containerships with capacities of 9,000+ TEUs are already under contract. Private-sector railroads, addressing supply chain competition and ports' needs to accommodate commercial and military cargo simultaneously, have employed double-stacked trains. Double-stacked trains require larger facilities for increased rail traffic, and higher tunnel and bridge clearances than currently exist in some areas. These requirements have renewed discussions about public/private rail investment in equipment and facilities in and near our ports.

2. Dual Use Issues

Introduction of new terminal technologies that enhance and improve just-in-time delivery processes within the nation's supply chain, a projected doubling of throughput on the system, and providing needed maintenance on the current system will require both flexibility and massive new investments in intermodal transportation infrastructure. Simultaneously, the intermodal system must be ready to adapt to a military deployment that moves simultaneously with commercial shipments. However, shipments through the intermodal system for military deployments are likely to include unusual cargo that requires special handling and more stringent security.

---

[12] National Chamber Foundation, "Trade and Transportation: A Study of North American Port and Intermodal Systems", U.S. Chamber of Commerce, Washington, DC, 2003, p. 1.

A top priority for military mobilization planners is to deliver combat units to the theatre of war as a complete fighting unit. Loading of combat units requires substantial staging areas for vehicles and aircraft, adequate port rail infrastructure, and port labor that is skilled in handling non-containerized military equipment. Therefore, the effectiveness of military cargo operations at the ports is directly tied to the quality of the mobility planning process and the availability of staging areas and rail infrastructure for sequencing of such equipment arriving from military bases around the country.

In contrast, commercial cargo is primarily containerized and unit integrity is generally not a shipper concern. As U.S. ports continue to expand their operations to meet the forecasted growth in commercial containerized freight, non-containerized facilities needed to support the unique military cargo handling requirements will become scarcer. This may reduce the ability of U.S. ports to facilitate future military unit deployments, such as OIF.

F. The Security Imperative

The vulnerability of our nation's ports to security threats and terrorism has prompted intense efforts to protect our maritime infrastructure since the September 11th terrorist attacks. However, at the same time that ports are being called upon to tighten their security, they are also moving ever-increasing volumes of commercial traffic, and some are also supporting military operations overseas. These demands present challenges and opportunities. The new security imperative will be an everyday challenge for transportation providers and ports, in terms of operations and resources, until security is integrated into everyday operations, as shown in Figure 4. The goal of both industry and the government is to protect the nation against the catastrophic impact of a terrorist act and at the same time not hamper the efficient flow of trade, which would disrupt the nation's economy.

Figure 4

The Security Imperative

Military Intermodal Use

Commercial Intermodal

Port & Intermodal Security in a Post-9/11 World

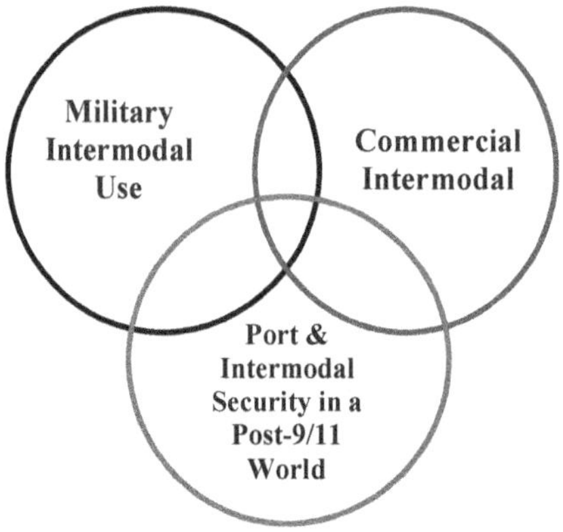

Source Trade and Transportation, 2003

To date, ports have completed risk assessments on the vulnerabilities of their facilities, proposed security measures to ameliorate those risks, and have started implementing and paying for them. These measures include security personnel for gates and patrols, fencing, lighting, cameras, and other surveillance measures such as inspection requirements, radiation detection, and cargo tracking.

Through FY 2004, ports have received over $515 million in Federal grant funding for port security measures. The total security expenditures that ports have made to date are not known at this time. However, it is estimated by the U.S. Coast Guard (USCG) that port facility security costs to meet mandated Maritime Transportation Security Act of 2002 (MTSA) regulations will be $5.4 billion over the next ten years, with $1.125 billion needed in calendar years 2004-2005.[13]

In accordance with MTSA regulations, facilities, including all the ports discussed in this report, were required to submit Facility Security Plans to the USCG for review and approval. As of July 1, 2004, each facility was required to implement its approved plan. The costs and resultant changes to the logistics chain from the plans' requirements and other mandated security requirements present an evolving scenario, and they are diverting port capacity and modernization investment resources away from commerce to security.

---

[13] Coast Guard, 33 CFR Parts 101 and 102, Implementation of National Maritime Security Initiatives, Temporary interim rule, *Federal Register* (Vol. 68, No. 126), July 1, 2003, page 39273.

This Page Intentionally Blank

Chapter II.   Analysis of Reported Operations and Challenges

A. Data Collection

During February 2004, information needed to assess intermodal efficiency and port performance was collected directly from key port, terminal, stevedore, and labor representatives at 23 ports by four MARAD-led DOT intermodal teams. Discussions at the outreach sessions focused on the performance of major components of the intermodal system: waterside, port/terminal intermodal interface, and landside movements. The site visits included the ten commercial ports that participated in the early OIF deployment.

Site visits were necessary because port statistics that might be used to measure port efficiency are highly variable between ports, and, because of competitive pressures, some information is considered to be commercially sensitive and generally not available to MARAD. The U.S. Government does not systematically collect port productivity data because U.S. ports are private or local government entities. For purposes of this Report, MARAD collected port specific information from other sources, including DOD, commercial shippers, and previous reports.

MARAD developed a set of structured questions to address port conditions, identify the sources of port congestion and suggest possible remedies, if needed. The DOT teams asked the same questions of each entity at each port. Additional questions were asked of ports that participated in OIF. A list of all questions appears in Appendix B. MARAD did not seek to collect information on the deficiencies of port management or labor practices. Rather, the collected information is a snapshot of the current congestion conditions in the U.S. intermodal system and their impact on military deployments.

The DOT teams focused on two separate operating scenarios of the MTS: normal commercial traffic, and the unique requirements of a military deployment through commercial ports. Information on commercial operations was obtained from all 23 ports; military deployments were discussed in depth only with the strategic commercial ports. This report discusses the top three intermodal obstacles identified by each of the 23 ports. For the most part, individual ports are not specified because of competitive business concerns. Therefore, areas of concern are discussed on an aggregate level in this report.

The issues and concerns that ports raised with MARAD during the site visits have been independently confirmed in other public sector, academic and industry reviews, studies and analyses of the intermodal system. There have been a significant number of surveys and reports completed in the last decade that indicate that continued enhancement of productivity of the MTS must be a focused national objective rather than the loose amalgamation of activities and institutions, that currently exists. These reports and results of other MARAD survey results are discussed in Appendix C.

B. Significant Areas of Concern for Both Commercial Port Operations and Military Deployments

The greatest concerns for both commercial operations and military deployments were the surge in cargo flows into the ports, the adequacy of cargo staging areas in the ports, port rail infrastructure, and communications. Additional issues that dominated commercial operations were landside access to ports, highway signage, channel and port dredging, increasing cargo volumes, financing, and intermodal connectivity. Two additional major concerns specific to military deployments were training and coordination among ports and shippers.

1. Cargo Surge

Peak cargo flows are a source of delay when rail and truck access to and within the ports is overloaded. While a sign of economic prosperity, seasonal increases put additional demands on the ports for cargo staging areas, requiring more longshore labor and exacerbating bottlenecks. Rail is especially impacted at peak season, when congested rail traffic frequently must wait at railway sidings used for pass zones thus increasing shipment delays. Minor rail breakdowns often result in even further congestion. The rail infrastructure at the marine terminals or on port property is generally antiquated and in many places cannot support a large surge of commercial cargo without significant delays. Twelve of 23 ports expressed a concern that they have some difficulty with their rail access. The ports of Savannah, Beaumont, Corpus Christi, and Houston reported significant rail delays, especially during peak season. Typical rail congestion issues involve rail cars that block other vehicular traffic, or vessel delays while waiting for the shoreside staging areas to clear.

The ports recognize this problem and several port authorities are embarking on locally funded improvement programs. However, in all cases these improvement programs are not seen as enough to meet current commercial surges or future defense needs. Ports in the peak pre-Christmas season on the West Coast and during the agricultural export season in the Gulf of Mexico, experience congestion problems such as trucks idling outside gates, rail heads jamming with simultaneous shipments, and rail cars blocking street intersections or other vehicles. Similarly, truck and rail crews awaiting entry or exit from ports find they are challenged by the new mandatory limits on hours of service.

The addition of military mobilization to normal commercial operations dramatically stresses the freight transportation system and severely tests its capability. Both strategic and non-strategic commercial port operators maintain infrastructure based on their normal commercial requirements and generally there is little excess capacity. During deployments, the increased demand placed on infrastructure capacity is met by using existing excess commercial capacity and by balancing the military needs with the commercial workload. Problems occur when the military requirement for capacity is greater than the excess commercial capacity available at the time of deployment. Prior to OIF, rail infrastructure was enhanced at a number of major U.S. Army bases by the U.S. Army's Strategic Mobility Program (ASMP), enabling the U.S. Army to deploy 5 1/3 divisions in 75 days.

The Ports of Jacksonville, Beaumont, and Corpus Christi noted that the increased rail throughput capability and the heavy push of loaded rail cars out of U.S. Army bases caused short-term rail congestion in the ports. This congestion rippled through the rail system and temporarily degraded cargo security. In some instances, military trains were left on rail sidings between U.S. Army bases and the ports. Port rail infrastructure shortfalls could become more serious in the future as trade grows and larger military deployments are required, or if the deployment occurs during peak commercial cargo shipment seasons. The strategic ports recognize this problem and are embarking on locally and Federally funded improvement programs.

2. Staging Area

Lack of adequate staging areas is a serious problem during times of peak cargo flow. Adding new staging capacity is difficult because competition for waterfront real estate is intense, and competing uses make it very difficult to acquire suitable new land. Additionally, expansion and land acquisition is expensive for the local port authority. Pressure for diversified use of waterfront real estate is expected to continue. As trade increases in the future, ports will need to expand or change their operations to provide staging areas that meet commercial needs, as well as to handle the military's unique equipment requirements in a deployment. Ports will first expand into existing under-utilized staging areas, and secondly, will look to new areas for expansion.

Ports are utilizing innovative techniques to handle current terminal congestion and land shortages. In some cases, empty containers must be stored on needed terminal space for staging cargo. Various approaches are used, including stacking containers higher, storing containers in production centers outside the port, and moving port business offices out of the port area to make more room. On a number of occasions during these site visits, the data collection teams received requests for a guide on best practice measures, including handling empty containers, extending gate hours, and updating terminal equipment. Those interviewed shared significant interest in easing congestion during peak cargo flows by using information technology to signal that a port could accept additional cargo, rather than having the shippers simply send the cargo.

3. Landside Access

Congestion is often a serious problem on highway approaches near the ports. Truck access to and from the National Highway System remains an issue in many places. Los Angeles, Savannah, Norfolk, and Houston provided specific examples of difficulties with near terminal truck traffic, especially during peak shipping seasons. Roadway improvements are needed in major metropolitan road corridors (e.g., I-10 in Texas and I-710 in California) to handle both private vehicles and commercial port cargoes. For example, truck lines up to 50 vehicles long were reported in some ports during the busiest seasons.

4. Port Rail Infrastructure

Rail shipments are also experiencing serious congestion problems. The Ports of Savannah, Beaumont, Corpus Christi and Houston reported significant rail delays, especially during peak season. Common impediments for rail included: low overpass bridges that restrict specific rail cars; the availability of single track/single operator port service that cannot address both commercial and military deployment priorities; and mainline rail terminals and yards that are distant from ports and necessitate moving large amounts of freight through populated areas. Additionally, 25 percent of the ports indicated that on-dock rail handling facilities are virtually nonexistent or inadequate at certain terminals.

5. Waterside Access – Channel and Port Dredging

Maintenance dredging is one of the most important infrastructure challenges for many ports. Several ports expressed concern that the U.S. Army Corps of Engineers has not received adequate funding to handle needed (and congressionally authorized) maintenance and improvement dredging projects. For example, the Gulf Intracoastal Waterway System was specifically mentioned as an area needing attention.

6. Increasing Trade Volumes – A Source of Congestion

The Ports of Los Angeles, Long Beach, Oakland, Houston, Savannah, and Charleston all reported intermodal cargo volumes exceeding forecasts, resulting in congestion. The ports emphasized that they are experiencing higher than projected cargo growth. They are aggressively responding to these cargo growth patterns which stress their current capacities. Houston is planning an entire new port terminal area (Bayport) to handle overflow cargo from the one million containers-per-year Barbour's Cut Terminal. New Orleans just opened a state of the art electronic terminal, and Oakland is considering relieving container congestion by shipping more containers inland by rail.

The growth in container volume causes additional ripple effects throughout the intermodal cargo movement chain. For example, empty containers accumulate; containers are held due to foreign biologic restrictions (Avian Flu/BSE-Mad Cow Disease), and containers awaiting pick-up take up space. A very few ports are charging increased fees (demurrage) for containers left in port after a grace period. Although such measures have raised some funds for the port, they have not helped the congestion problem. Ports have asked for: Federal planning to identify best practices in improving port productivity with limited land area, and for the elimination of choke points (such as at terminal gates and rail interfaces) with a wide variety of stakeholders and agencies. The port director of Savannah, Georgia, who saw a 60 percent surge in container traffic (25 percent of the new customers stayed on after the congestion situation cleared) said, "I have been in the port maritime business for 30 years, this is the first time the Federal Government has asked the ports about how they were doing …their [government] interest is welcomed and encouraged."

7. Finance

Many ports indicated that increased state and Federal funding would be helpful. One Texas port representative's answer was typical. The port is trying to fix its rail infrastructure with general tax revenue bonds that compete locally for school improvement financing and other needed projects. The specific port in question is in an air quality non-attainment area and will provide matching funds to participate in an $8 million Federal Congestion Mitigation Air Quality cost share program available in TEA-21 to improve rail access. Unfortunately, the basic need is for $15 million to attain adequate air quality. Ports also indicated that they need training in the various port financing instruments available to reduce pressure on general obligation bond requirements. Finally, mandatory security costs have an impact on infrastructure budgets, taking away from needed improvements.

8. Highway Signage

In general, port terminals and access routes are not clearly marked from the highway. This causes disruption and delayed shipments. To mitigate signage problems, Seattle has produced a port guidebook for new drivers, as have some other ports. New Orleans has special AM radio stations assisting drivers in getting to the ports. These and other solutions should be adopted by all ports.

9. Connectivity

Rail infrastructure connections at our nation's ports are often privately held. Therefore, they present special challenges for coordination with the Class One rail carriers.[14] New Orleans is building a new rail traffic control station to coordinate the activities of the six Class One rail systems that serve the port. Most ports do not have such a system. Consequently, ports are often faced with competing demands for the same rail track, or find themselves in a market in which all shippers rush rail cargo to market simultaneously (e.g., grain season) causing systemic rail congestion "from Kansas to Texas" during peak seasons.

10. Communications

Ports and terminals are sometimes confronted with unexpected lines of trucks at the gate, or a unit train (several dozen rail cars) arriving unannounced. This can occur because cargo owners and freight forwarders frequently do not communicate their daily requirements to the rail carriers and ports. This creates immediate port congestion, limits operational flexibility, and makes recovery difficult, as the ports do not have enough time to call out longshore gangs or make staging area arrangements.

Port communication with railroads was often cited as an example of "non-infrastructure" congestion. Placing the added burden of a military mobilization on this system can mean the congestion becomes unmanageable. When the DOT teams asked the railroads about the value of periodic teleconferencing with their customers to improve planning, they indicated that they were willing to talk with the DOD and commercial shippers on this issue.

Several ports mentioned that communications among the Federal agencies within the port were also a cause of delay. Several ports mentioned that this condition resulted in congestion. For example, they believe the local U.S. Department of Agriculture (USDA) inspector should be communicating with the local border and transportation services representatives, and the U.S. local Citizenship and Immigration Services. Another concern was communication from Federal agency headquarters to their field offices on standard inspection procedures and the need for consistency. The data collection teams were told that if one port inspector is found to be significantly more difficult than

---

[14] According to the Association of American Railroads - Policy and Economics Department, January 9, 2004, Class I Railroad Statistics (http://www.aar.org/PubCommon/Documents/AboutTheIndustry/Statistics.pdf), Class One Railroads are defined as line haul freight railroads with operating revenue in excess of $272.0 million. In 2003, the Class One railroads were: The Burlington Northern and Santa Fe Railway, CSX Transportation, Grand Trunk Corporation, Kansas City Southern Railway, Norfolk Southern Combined Railroad Subsidiaries, Soo Line Railroad, and Union Pacific Railroad.

others, a vessel operator may go "port shopping" for an easier port to use. This may occur if the operator is not heavily invested in a particular port.

With regard to communications requirements for a deployment, all the strategic commercial ports used in OIF indicated that the communication infrastructure is sufficient during normal commercial operations but is not robust enough to handle the increased requirements during a major deployment or national emergency. This lack made it difficult for deployment stakeholders to communicate and coordinate cargo operations early in the deployment.

C. Significant Concerns for National Defense Deployment Operations

1. Assured Access to Strategic Ports

Strategic commercial ports, terminals, railroads, longshore labor, and trucking companies are not compensated for their non-mobilization readiness activities. In addition, terminals at the strategic commercial ports are subject to Port Planning Orders (PPOs) that make these facilities less attractive to potential lessees. Assured port access is vital to our national defense, but such access carries a price. Some have suggested that the Federal government provide financial incentives to assist the strategic ports in meeting their commitments under this program.

2. Training

Longshore labor and DOD have expressed concerns about not having a sufficient number of skilled laborers, especially skilled drivers for military equipment during OIF, to handle both commercial and military cargoes simultaneously. Currently, port readiness training is conducted by the Port Readiness Committees during port readiness exercises held every other year at the strategic commercial ports. In addition, MARAD and the American Association of Port Authorities conduct national port readiness workshops annually. DOD, through U.S. Army Forces Command, conducts Sea Emergency Deployment Readiness Exercises (SEDRE).
These exercises have been helpful in addressing systemic weaknesses and addressing local concerns in advance of an actual deployment.

3. Coordination

The lack of an in-transit cargo tracking capability required constant adjustments to cargo operations and greatly reduced port productivity and intermodal efficiencies early in the OIF deployment. As the deployment continued, the U.S. Transportation Command and the Surface Deployment and Distribution Command (SDDC) established daily port operations meetings and teleconferences with the U.S. Army bases, ports, and the railroads to coordinate cargo flow and provide in-transit visibility. The situation improved but remains an issue. Another factor that the ports believe contributed to early deployment confusion was a lack of understanding of the composition of the cargo to be deployed through the ports.

Chapter III. Department of Defense and Commercial Shipper Perspectives

Public ports have both military and commercial customers, and their requirements are often significantly different.

A. Department of Defense

For this report, MARAD requested and received information from General John W. Handy, Commander, U.S. Transportation Command (USTRANSCOM), SDDC, and SDDC's Transportation Engineering Agency (SDDC-TEA) on the assessment of seaports engaged in the OIF deployment. SDDC-TEA analyzed hundreds of final Situation Reports for CONUS deployments and other pertinent documents. From December 2002 through May 2003, SDDC coordinated the movement of over 18 million square feet of cargo on approximately 200 vessels. Over 18,000 ammunition shipments were moved to seaports. SDDC managed 50 stevedoring and related terminal service contracts/basic ordering agreements. There were 108,500 truck shipments to commercial seaports (including nearly 20,000 shipments of arms, ammunition, and explosives) among 547 motor carriers. There were 789 rail shipments, among 26 rail carriers, to commercial seaports.[15]

With regard to the high volume of cargo shipped via rail, SDDC indicated that daily teleconferences among all stakeholders facilitated problem resolution. Centralized control allowed prioritization of movement to prevent bottlenecks. Selecting military bases as power projection platforms for priority deployments greatly improved rail use for military operations compared to OPERATION DESERT SHIELD/STORM. However, SDDC noted that seaport infrastructure requires greater capacity to mirror the improved military power projection capabilities.

Although there was a reported instance of congestion that required a SDDC organization to relocate within a port, SDDC stated that, overall, the commercial seaports served our deployment needs admirably. While ports did their best to provide as much staging and pier space as possible, SDDC believes a more robust and definitive contractual type of agreement is needed to guarantee space and compensate the port for the expenses resulting from letting DOD move "to the head of the line." SDDC indicated that its use of Long Beach, in particular, was very positive due to the ability to use an unoccupied pier area.

Additionally, USTRANSCOM stated that congestion was a factor in the early stages of the deployment, but all parties adapted to the cargo flow and significant delays due to congestion were avoided. SDDC-TEA worked with the Federal Highway Administration and State Area Command Defense Movement Coordinators to ensure there were no public highway "show-stoppers." SDDC's port call messages coordinated the phased movement of cargo from the military installations through the ports. Daily conference calls between SDDC, railroads, seaports, military bases, and Combatant Commands facilitated coordination of issues and resolution of challenges.

Corpus Christi and Jacksonville supplemented labor pools with stevedore gangs from neighboring ports, plus hundreds of military personnel were provided to facilitate the operations. The Port of San Diego's labor shortages were more difficult to overcome. In the planning phase, operational

---

[15] Brigadier General Barbara Doornink, Deputy Commanding General and Director of Operations, speech at the American Association of Ports Authorities Spring Conference, March 25, 2003.

challenges such as scheduling straight stern ramp ships at piers that could accommodate them, ship channel limitations, and bridge height restrictions were successfully overcome.

Supplementing port labor with military Port Support Activity personnel (to drive unique pieces of equipment, for example) was important to the rapid flow of cargo. Through the cooperation of all parties, several other facility factors – areas for preparing aircraft for overseas movement, strength of the piers, lighting, medical assistance, crane availability, and truck reception capability – did not become significant issues because they were either provided or alternatives were developed to meet deployment needs.

Some military bases, selected for priority deployments, have significantly improved rail outloading capabilities and are now capable of loading and pulling 240 rail cars in a 24-hour period. Some ports require reception facilities – rail capacity and rail car switching infrastructure – to provide increased movement capability. Port rail car holding capacity and the ability to unload and remove empty rail cars are key to the efficient flow of cargo. This was of particular concern at Jacksonville, Beaumont, and Corpus Christi where there was a high volume of rail activity. However, the ports worked through those operational constraints.

In testimony before the Senate Armed Services Subcommittee on Seapower on March 10, 2004, General Handy stated, "Our readiness also depends on timely access to militarily useful commercial transportation."[16] USTRANSCOM has also indicated to MARAD that port congestion, to varying degrees, affected the shipment of DOD cargo during OIF. Port authorities faced increased economic costs, maintaining commitments to their customers and competing demands for space. These factors resulted in space shortages for DOD cargo at some locations, such as the competing set of demands that occurred at San Diego and Norfolk during OIF. If a requirement to move large amounts of military unit cargo had developed at a major commercial container port, such as Oakland or the Port of New York/New Jersey, this issue would have been more significant. Consistent with the National Chamber Foundation of the U.S. Chamber of Commerce study and MARAD's communication with USTRANSCOM, MARAD expects that the following major DOD trends will continue:

- DOD deployment will depend largely upon adequate commercial infrastructure being available;
- Defense and commercial supply chains will become more integrated;
- Deployment timeframes will be more ambitious;
- Peacetime sensitivity to safety and security issues will increase; and
- The dual-use national intermodal freight system will have to be ready to respond to a full spectrum of crises.

Despite DOD efforts to shrink the geographic footprint of its deployment needs for freight transportation, the transition challenge for ports from business-as-usual will become more difficult. As discussed in the previous chapter, the results of the DOT team interviews at the strategic ports used during the OIF deployment show that the marine component and the landside intermodal components of the intermodal freight system performed well under OIF's additional demands. However, as we look to the future, there is no doubt that rapid deployments will place additional

---

[16] Testimony of General John W. Handy , Commander of USTRANSCOM on March 10, 2004 before Seapower Subcommittee of the Senate Armed Forces Committee.

burdens on a marine and intermodal system that is already under stress, a situation that will be exacerbated by the growing trade volume. Within the last two years, the freight system supported military operations in Iraq, Afghanistan, Korea, Bosnia, Kosovo, and Haiti; we must be prepared for other future deployments.

B. Commercial Shippers

MARAD, as part of its outreach efforts, met with leaders of trade associations that represent the interests of the commercial transportation providers within the port system framework. This meeting included the American Association of Port Authorities (AAPA), the Association of American Railroads (AAR), the American Trucking Associations (ATA), the Intermodal Association of North America (IANA), the World Shipping Council (representing U.S. and foreign flag vessel operators), the American Association of State Highway and Transportation Officials (AASHTO), and others. While these groups represent a broad spectrum of transportation interests, they were united in their recognition that congestion is a serious concern for the U.S. port and freight system. The discussion focused on the following common concerns:

1. A Lack of Public Awareness of the Needs of the Transport System

The phrase "Freight Doesn't Vote" is often used to denote the fact that freight congestion does not register with decision-makers. Commercial shippers believe that the people of the United States, and the Federal Government by extension, are not seen as active enough in calling for the removal of national freight transportation impediments that have a negative impact on their everyday lives. Conversely, a representative of the World Shipping Council indicated that the Netherlands and Singapore governments recognize the contributions to the economy and quality of life that effective port operations make. In the next few years Singapore, with government support, will grow to have as much container throughput capacity as the entire United States. Similarly, it was mentioned that the Federal Government in the Netherlands typically takes a one-third stake in major port expansion projects, such as the new land reclamation project in Rotterdam now underway.

In the United States, transportation decisions are currently made at the local and state level. Politically and geographically, it has not made economic sense for a local community to use local dollars to fund projects to move more freight in and out of a port. In some cases, it has taken over ten years just to get the "last mile"[17] of highway connected to intermodal facilities, including ports.

2. The U.S. Needs To Increase Freight Transportation System Capacity

Historically, transportation planning, funding and operation have been made by each transportation mode (i.e., highway, air, rail, and marine). Since the transportation system is now at capacity in many places, freight and passenger transportation issues need to be addressed from a system-wide perspective in order to maximize solutions. This stakeholder group believes the DOT should provide the needed leadership. Private sector innovations, such as mega-container ships, may cause efficiencies in some areas but result in increased congestion in others. One of the world's largest containerships, the SUSAN MAERSK, can carry over 6,000 TEUs of cargo and is a major transportation event on arrival in any port. Today, vessels are already being contracted for with

---

[17] The "last mile" is defined as the construction of approaches to port facilities that connect to the Nation Highway System. The "last mile" is often a major choke point in and out of a port.

capacities of over 9,000 TEUs. Ports and surface transportation communities must plan for strategies to support the new "economies of scale" being asked for in the market place, yet they believe there is no forum to help break down the modal transportation planning barriers. Growing landside congestion at U.S. ports will also have an impact on the international competitiveness of the United States and must be addressed.

In addition to recommending additional dedicated funding for intermodal connectors from the Federal government, some of the commercial stakeholders' recommendations include looking at expanded gate access times, use of technology, and the application of new ideas, such as short sea shipping to relieve congestion. They recommended that transportation and port issues be addressed systemically. Just as we understand a river's watershed – where the water comes from and the need to maintain its quality and flow – we should approach broad transportation public policy issues systemically.

3. Security Concerns Are Draining Resources Away From Needed Infrastructure

Since the terrorist attacks of September 11th, port and freight security requirements have become crucial. However, every possible attempt should be made to balance the needs of security and commerce, with the goal that port and freight security systems be non-intrusive, facilitate trade, and not be funded entirely by the commercial and local service providers. Ports and service providers are seeing funds that normally would have been made available for needed port infrastructure projects being diverted to security measures. Ports have spent millions of dollars to upgrade security, and they spend many thousands of dollars per day more when the Department of Homeland Security threat advisory level is raised. These investment funds diverted to important security needs mean that funding to meet projected freight volume growth is diminishing at the very time when such investments must be made to keep our economy competitive in the global economy.

Service providers are also concerned about effects of the full complement of security measures (e.g., container security, the Transportation Worker Identification Card (TWIC), and port security plans) on congestion, efficiency and economics. The stakeholders recommended that the government supply some equity to make up for the loss in infrastructure funds, and to listen to the ports and service providers fully before implementing far-reaching and intrusive security mandates. For example, certain types of electronic devices on containers would greatly reduce the time needed to locate an individual container within a stack.

4. Commercial Stakeholders Summary Recommendations

- Address transportation issues from a global perspective;

- New concepts and technology should be used to reduce port congestion; and

- The Federal government should fund a greater share of the costs of security improvements so the ports do not have to divert funds from capital improvement projects.

Chapter IV.   Future Issues

The current challenges faced by the nation's intermodal freight transportation system from commercial pressures and military rapid deployment requirements were analyzed in previous chapters. Transportation stakeholders provided input regarding infrastructure impediments and impacts as they related to OIF. This chapter addresses transportation issues that have an impact on the future of our nation's Marine Transportation System. Although much of what must be done to meet these challenges will require years to complete, such as infrastructure repair and replacement, these improvements will generate increased rounds of economic activity, including creation of jobs. The challenges that face our nation's MTS and proposals to strengthen it are being considered by the Executive Branch, the Congress, and private-sector interests.[18]

A. Existing Capacity Available To Meet Future Challenges

Many of the challenges to be met by our commercial port and intermodal systems are already apparent, and the port and other industries that are part of the MTS have recognized and called attention to intermodal impediments over the years. Twenty years ago, the port industry proposed the establishment of an "Intermodal Truck-Rail Container Transfer Facility" to maintain productivity in the Los Angeles/Long Beach ports in anticipation of the advent of 3,000 TEU vessels. This intermodal rail facility was conceived to accommodate up to eight unit trains simultaneously and would be positioned within 2.5 miles to the port terminals of the San Pedro Bay ports of Los Angeles and Long Beach. However, today's larger vessels of 8,000 TEUs or more can require over 20 unit trains to serve the import and export demands of the Ports of Los Angeles and Long Beach, far exceeding the projections of the demands for port throughput.

Recently, ship-owners have contracted with foreign shipyards for new container vessels with capabilities exceeding 9,000 TEUs. Moreover, current advances in ship propulsion and hull design could lead to even larger containerships within the next two decades. The twenty year planning horizon and the statistical analysis tools used may need to be re-evaluated to ensure that they are in sync with the new global realities of economic interdependence, rapidly changing trade patterns and the technological advances in naval architecture and engine designs.

As a means to continue maintaining port productivity over the past decade, development of "on-dock" and "near-dock" intermodal transfer facilities within the San Pedro Bay ports have led to the creation of the Alameda Transportation Corridor. The Corridor currently handles over 250 unit trains weekly moving from the West Coast of the United States to the Midwest and East Coast. Even as these remedies are implemented, growth is outstripping capacity. Freight shipments are projected to grow 400 percent by 2020 for Los Angeles and Long Beach.

National economies are already globally connected and interdependent, which benefits the U.S. International trade is an increasing part of our economy. For example, U.S. international trade in goods had a value of $1.046 trillion in 1993. In 2003, international trade amounted to over $ 2.0

---

[18] Recent reports and studies from diverse sources such as: the National Chamber Foundation of the U.S. Chamber of Commerce, the Marine Board of the Transportation Research Board of the National Academies, the Marine Transportation System National Advisory Council, the Government Accountability Office, and the U.S. Commission on Ocean Policy.

trillion, an increase of almost 90 percent in 11 years.[19] Over the next decade, the value of international cargo will increase through our port gateways, and our national economy will be inexorably linked to this trade. Granted, there will be annual fluctuations in trade, but the long-term trend of substantial growth will continue.

Currently there is sufficient port capacity in the nation's coastal regions, as shown in Figure 5. Without exception, all 23 ports included in this study are likely to experience an increase of at least one-third over their current traffic volumes in the next ten years, based upon continued freight growth of 3 to 4 percent per year. The results of the National Chamber Foundation of the U.S. Chamber of Commerce's Trade and Transportation Study projected even higher rates of growth. That study found that 14 of the 16 ports (88 percent) analyzed will experience at least a 50 percent increase in container traffic.[20]

Figure 5

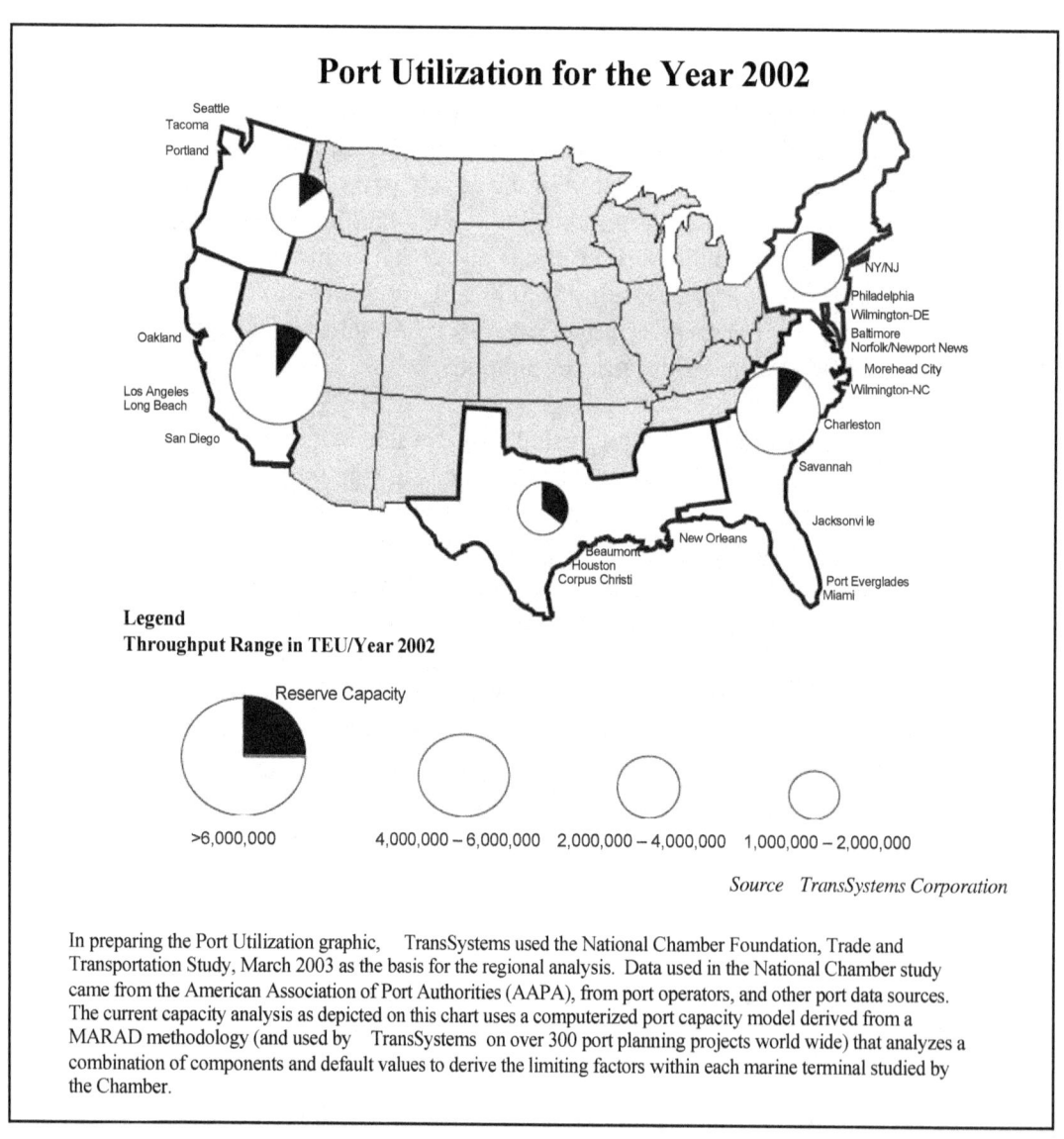

---

[19] Source: "U.S. International Trade in Goods and Services, Annual Revision for 2003," U.S. Department of Commerce, Bureau of Economic Analysis, Washington, DC, June 24, 2004.
[20] National Chamber Foundation, p. 6

B. Escalating Pressure: Demand for Port Capacity

Growth in trade is not the only challenge that ports will face in meeting future demand. Figure 6 illustrates the array of escalating pressures to which ports are subjected, in addition to freight growth.

Figure 6

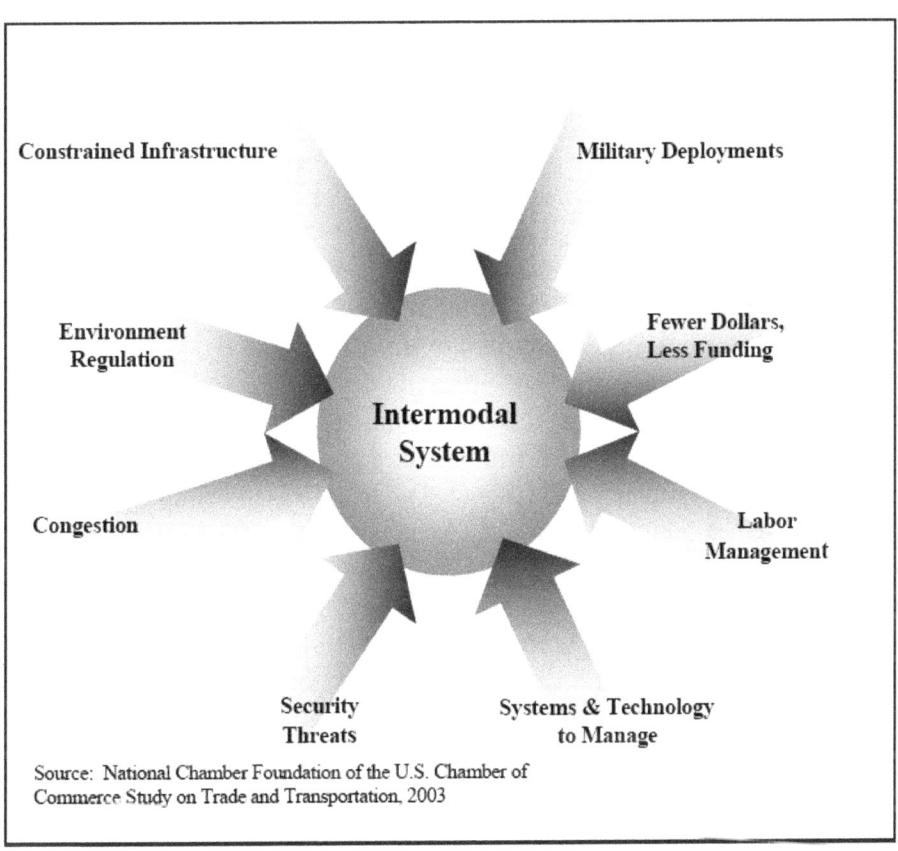

Source: National Chamber Foundation of the U.S. Chamber of Commerce Study on Trade and Transportation, 2003

In the future there will be more freight moving. As larger ships put increased pressure on our ports, greater container volumes and customer expectations will require an effective, efficient, and integrated total transportation solution. The future 9,000+ TEU vessels and their associated gateway port volumes will: require marine terminals that maximize facility throughput with unparalleled reliability; use intermodal rail to a much greater extent than today; dramatically reduce operating costs; employ state-of-the-art technology, such as advanced in-transit visibility; and reduce life-cycle costs.

America's port and intermodal freight system is rapidly approaching capacity limits, with growing congestion in metropolitan areas and passenger/freight corridors. A recent study found that urban congestion, exacerbated by increased movements of freight, already costs consumers $70 billion per year in wasted time and fuel.[21]

---

[21] Texas Transportation Institute, Texas A&M University System, The 2003 Annual Urban Mobility Report, September 2003, p. iii.

There are warning signs that our national intermodal system may not be able to keep up with commercial and military challenges:

- **Intermodal Connectivity** – Intermodal infrastructure is fragmented and lacks a fully integrated system. National policies needed to create truly seamless transportation connections are still in the development stage.

- **Information Systems** – Information systems used by one mode of transportation are not fully compatible with those used in other modes.

- **Labor** – Longshore labor and intermodal management do not always work together to develop a coordinated approach to port congestion problems or to facilitate integration of the latest technologies, most advanced equipment or best practices that can improve port efficiency.

- **Terminal Productivity** – American ports lag well behind other international transportation gateways such as Singapore and Rotterdam in terms of productivity.

- **Intermodal Improvements** – The U.S. does not focus on intermodal improvements when planning for long term highway infrastructure projects. At the same time, railroad infrastructure, which is similarly capital-intensive and time-consuming, is totally funded through the private capital investment of railroad companies.

Massive investments in facility modernization and increasing freight capacity already underway at key ports around the world are also a warning sign of the need for increased U.S. capacity to efficiently handle major freight growth. Because the United States accounts for 20 percent in global trade, expansion in foreign ports is a leading indicator of the increased volume of trade that will funnel through our seaports into our nation's economy. For example:

- the Port of Shanghai is spending $6.9 billion in order to achieve an annual container capacity of 25 million TEUs by 2010;
- the Port of Rotterdam is spending approximately $2.5 billion to expand its container capacity from 6.2 million TEUs to an estimated 8 million TEUs by 2008; and,

- the Port of Singapore's expansion ($7 billion on one terminal alone) is expected to raise its container capacity by 18 million TEUs, for a total of 35 million TEUs by 2009.

U.S. container capacity (approximately 27 million TEUs per year) is not growing at the same pace as that of international ports. Thus, in five years, just one foreign port – Singapore – will have more container capacity than all the combined U.S. ports have today. Increased imports without corresponding growth in port capacity will lead to more congestion and inefficiencies in our intermodal system that will hamper economic growth, job creation, and the global competitiveness of the U.S. economy.

While domestic waterborne trade is expected to grow modestly, U.S. international container traffic is projected to at least double from 2001 to 2020. Some ports will experience even more rapid growth. For example, the Port Authority of New York and New Jersey expects that its cargo will double by 2013 and triple by 2020. Intermodal demand is expected to grow by 25 percent in just five years. In the near term, U.S. ports will be able to meet the demand. However, at current growth rates, there will be shortfalls of port capacity in all regions of the country by 2010, as shown in Figure 7

Figure 7

Port Capacity Shortfall Forecast for the Year 2010

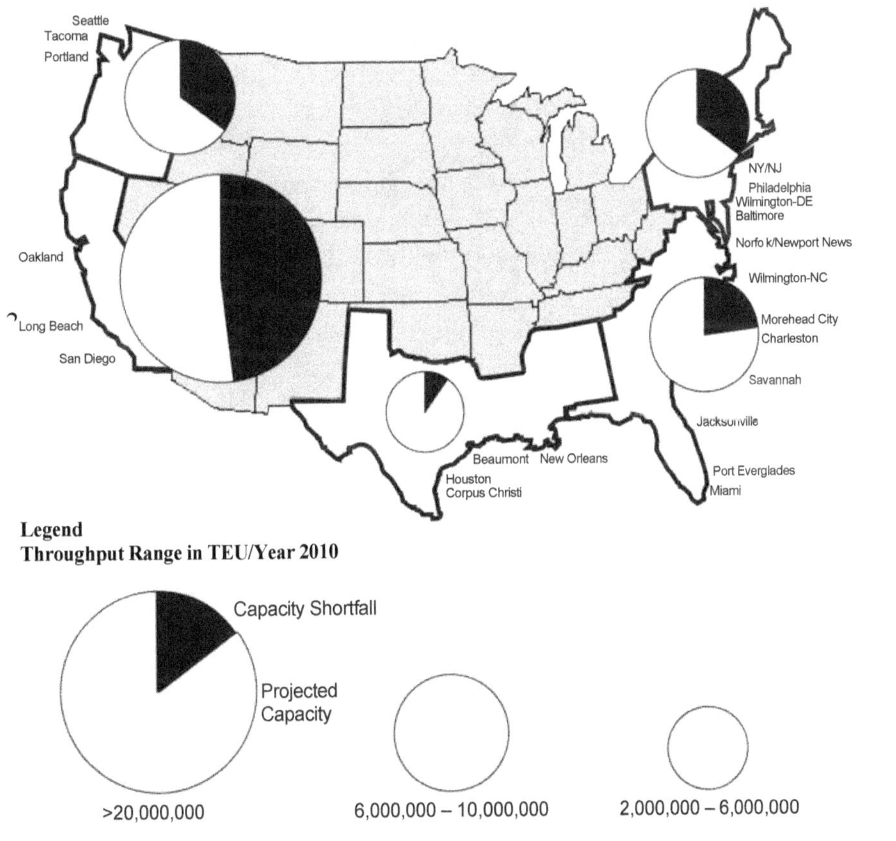

Legend
Throughput Range in TEU/Year 2010

Capacity Shortfall

Projected Capacity

>20,000,000   6,000,000 – 10,000,000   2,000,000 – 6,000,000

Source TransSystems Corporation

In preparing the Cargo Forecast and Capacity Shortfall, TransSystems used the National Chamber Foundation, Trade and Transportation Study, March 2003 as the bases for the regional data. Baseline volumes were developed for each of the ports within the Chamber Study and the volumes were segmented by trade route and direction, allowing the team to develop macro drivers for each region of the county. These macro drivers were then applied to the individual ports by market segment and trade route to develop a forecasted growth for each port within the study.

C. Future Growth of Port Capacity

In the near-term, the ports will continue to manage congestion by using innovative ways to optimize use. However, new physical terminal capacity is not the only requirement. Our entire intermodal transportation system must provide better ways of moving cargo in and out of the ports.

1. Technological Advances for More Efficient Port Utilization

Southern California Ports have plans underway to make their ports "agile" by using "sprint trains" to take intermodal cargo directly from dockside and move it to a remote inland location for storage and sorting prior to distribution. This promises to significantly increase productivity. Agile port demonstration projects at the Ports of Tacoma and Philadelphia are encouraging efforts at synchronizing ship and inland intermodal freight information across the modes.

These innovative, or agile port systems, could have significant military deployment benefits as well. For example, large quantities of material and the associated square footage required must be moved "from fort to port." An optimized intermodal military freight system would allow rapid, synchronized deployment from inland depots to any port on any coast for military debarkation using just in time services already highly developed in the commercial economy. However, the important issue is not technology, but rather that a unified joint action freight information system be developed and coordinated between all of the modes of carriage.

Such projects could greatly increase cargo capacity on the same waterfront acreage without the necessity of new construction, new equipment or changes in labor. Even with these measures, the surplus capacity that is available today will soon be fully utilized.

Dedicated intermodal freight corridors will be needed for distribution well beyond city limits. Already, the Ports of Los Angeles and Long Beach are planning to extend the Alameda Corridor east of the metropolitan area. However, such projects face some key challenges to future expansion.

2. Key Challenges to Future Port Expansion

Our nation's MTS is a key factor in economic growth and already faces significant challenges. Based on meetings with the ports, stevedores, terminal operators, labor, and reviews of other reports, MARAD has identified a number of key issues:

a. Developable Land for Port Operations

- During the DOT team port interviews, ports said that they still have room to grow, especially in the Gulf Coast regions, but the space is unevenly distributed. Some ports and terminal operators indicated that while the current land was sufficient, the terminals were poorly laid out and caused congestion. Poor use of existing land is just as much a problem as lack of developable land. As we get closer to 2020, the required port expansion will begin to use up the developable land available today. Environmental issues, for example, will almost certainly be a constant cause of delay in the future, just as they are today. Better planning and coordination among all entities with an interest in port development and a streamlined approval process are mandatory if the United States desires to accommodate the projected growth in intermodal shipping.

- The U.S. Chamber of Commerce and others have supported these findings that land constraints (fueled by population growth in coastal states and around ports) and environmental restrictions will soon limit the expansion of our largest ports, putting a premium on efficient intermodal connectors, particularly urban freight hubs and high-volume corridors.

b. Waterside Access

- During the DOT team port interviews, channel depth was raised as a significant concern. For example, the 6,600 TEU SUSAN MAERSK, one of the largest containerships to call in the United Sates, requires a channel depth of 44 feet (14.5 meters). There are only six U.S. mainland container ports that have the depth, facilities and access to markets necessary to support direct vessel calls by this generation of containerships.

- During the port interviews, DOT team members were told that the existing depth at most ports is adequate. However, some are already operating at maximum draft levels. At least one port in the U.S. South Atlantic has limited berthing hours to high tide. As the U.S. Army Corps of Engineers dredging backlog continues, the number of ports with limited berthing hours will increase. Without a concerted effort to deepen and maintain channel depths, the United States will not be able to handle routinely the new generation of container vessels. Since these vessels are already in production, the ship owners will seek trade routes with harbors in other nations that are already deep enough to handle larger vessels, or establish a feeder service to the United States.

- Linear limits of berthing were also raised as a waterside access issue. Terminal operators seem to be more aware of the need for both depth and increased berthing space than the ports themselves. However, as containership capacity increases, so does the vessel's length and breadth. In the future, linear berthing limits, crane reaches and channel depth, will become more significant.

- It was also mentioned that new equipment, such as specialized cranes, to serve modern containerships would be required in the future.

- Larger vessels off-load larger volumes of cargo that must be moved through our ports, increasing congestion, and creating bottlenecks and choke points throughout our entire intermodal transportation system. As the larger containerships of the future are deployed, these conditions will be exacerbated and addressing these impediments will become even more urgent and costly.

- Despite a comprehensive strategy by the U.S. Army Corps of Engineers to reduce the construction backlog of maintenance and improvement projects on our waterways and their associated elements, there are currently over $11 billion in construction projects that remain to be addressed.[22]

- In 2003, 53 percent of the locks and dams operated by the U.S. Army Corps of Engineers were over 50 years old, and many are too small for efficient freight movement. The Inland Waterways Users Board stated that "the failure in past years to fund these projects at their optimum capability levels has already resulted in benefits foregone to our nation of $2.177 billion."[23] Opportunity costs will continue to increase unless maintenance and expansion of our inland waterways infrastructure is commensurate with the expected growth in trade. The Saint Lawrence Seaway faces similar structural challenges.

c. Road Access

- The ports and terminal operators interviewed by MARAD frequently mentioned road and highway congestion as a serious problem. Only a few of them limited their responses specifically to the "last mile."

- Many interviewees stated that motor carriers cannot handle the growth in freight without a massive new investment in highways and roads.

d. Rail Access

Poor or inadequate rail access was the most frequently mentioned infrastructure impediment mentioned during the DOT team port interviews. Many railroads are ill-equipped to handle larger volumes of freight because they cannot afford to privately fund the massive investments needed to keep pace with the demands that the expected trade growth will place on rail infrastructure.

---

[22] LTG Robert B. Flowers, Chief of Engineers, U.S. Army Corps of Engineers, "Testimony before the Subcommittee on Water Resources and Environment, Committee on Transportation and Infrastructure", U.S. House of Representatives, February 26, 2004, p. 4.
[23] Inland Waterways Users Board, _17th Annual Report to the Secretary of the Army and the United States Congress_, February 2003, pl. ES-1 and 3.

Chapter V.   Proposals for a New Federal Role: DOT Initiatives

For years our ports have had the local funding and the land on which to build in response to congestion. However, financial resources are becoming increasingly scarce while land development costs are growing at a geometric rate. Ports have to innovate in order to make the best use of these resources and still answer increased capability demands.

Ports, already facing substantial maintenance and investment requirements before the September 11th terrorist attacks, have been forced to divert substantial resources away from infrastructure projects in order to comply with new security requirements.[24] Port facility security costs, estimated by the Coast Guard to be $1.125 billion for calendar years 2004-2005 and $5.4 billion over the next decade, will continue to absorb resources necessary for infrastructure projects through this period.[25]

While ports do not advocate a national port system due to potential competitive impacts, they welcome Federal assistance in such areas as port-to-transportation system interfaces and security funding. Federal assistance to coordinate and assist in the development of transportation resources is clearly needed and desired by the port and terminal operators.

A. DOT's Systemic Approach to National Transportation Policy

Previous reports and studies point to a need for a systemic approach to national transportation policy that better coordinates expenditures for highways, public mass transit, rail, airports, and seaports. The transportation system can no longer afford to operate in a modally distinctive manner and be able to respond to system pressures. In addition to the volume and security challenge to the MTS, there are also 17 different Federal agencies in six cabinet level departments responsible for maritime decision making. In the past, this has led to a patchwork of inefficient laws, polices, and programs.

As the GAO found, "there is a growing awareness of, and agreement about, the need to view various transportation modes from an integrated standpoint, particularly for the purposes of developing and implementing a Federal investment strategy and alternative funding approach."[26]

There has been a single comprehensive program for surface transportation since 1991. SAFETEA is the Department's proposal for reauthorization of the surface transportation legislation. SAFETEA is awaiting Congressional action despite the fact that surface transportation legislation expired on September 30, 2003. The VISION 100 / Century of Aviation Reauthorization Act (PL108-176,) which funds comprehensive programs to strengthen the Federal aviation system, was signed into law by President Bush in December 2003. To date, there is not a comprehensive Federal program related to the Marine Transportation System, which is why the Administration continues to address the needs of the Marine Transportation/Maritime Industry using the targeted approach referred to in this Report.

---

[24] U.S. General Accounting Office, GAO-04-315R "Aviation and Port Security", December 2003, p. 3.

[25] Coast Guard, op. cit. page 13,

[26] United States General Accounting Office, Report to the Chairman, Subcommittee on Surface Transportation and Merchant Marine, Committee on Commerce Science, and Transportation, U.S. Senate, *Marine Transportation: Federal Financing and Framework for Infrastructure Investments* (Washington, DC, September 2002), p. 18.

Despite intermodal freight initiatives created by the 1991 Intermodal Surface Transportation Efficiency Act (ISTEA) and TEA-21, significant gaps still exist in programs, policies, and funding related to creating and maintaining the most efficient, seamless transportation system necessary to compete in the global economy. Responsibility for improving the intermodal freight system lies largely within the purview of DOT. In response, the Administration has proposed significant freight related initiatives in the Safe, Accountable, Flexible, and Efficient Transportation Equity Act of 2003 (SAFETEA) over the coming six years, including:

1. **Funding for Intermodal Connectors** – After conducting a survey of intermodal connectors and analyzing their conditions under ISTEA and TEA-21, the Administration's SAFETEA legislation proposes that a portion of each state's National Highway System (NHS) funds be dedicated for intermodal transportation projects. States are free to use these funds for other purposes if they can demonstrate that all the NHS intermodal connectors in their jurisdiction are in good condition.

2. **Credit Tools for Freight Investment** – SAFETEA will help to finance freight gateways, intermodal facilities, border crossing improvements, and expansion of multi-state trade corridor programs with two key provisions directed at freight projects.

    a. **Private Activity Bonds** – Exempt facility bonds issued for highway facilities and surface freight transfer facilities would not be subject to the annual volume cap for private activity bonds, but they may not exceed $15 billion in the aggregate. This promises to be an important tool for freight financing, which shares the cost obligation between the public and private sectors. It should be noted that marine ports and terminals are not eligible facilities or considered in SAFETEA's definition of an International Gateway.

    b. **The Transportation Infrastructure Finance and Innovation Act** (TIFIA) – TIFIA has been redefined to make it more accessible to smaller freight projects under SAFETEA. Freight rail projects can qualify for TIFIA loans, and the SAFETEA bill reduces the eligible project cost to $50 million from the $100 million level. It should be noted that TIFIA does not presently allow for seaport investment projects.

The following initiatives, which include marine freight issues in varying degrees, enhance planning capabilities by addressing freight challenges at the Federal, state and local levels:

1. **Capacity Building** – The Federal Highway Administration has launched a Freight Professional Capacity Building Program, and plans to significantly add to its scope under SAFETEA. This education and training effort is creating greater institutional awareness of freight issues for public transportation planners.

2. **Improved Planning** – States will be required to include intermodal issues in the planning process, and to establish freight transportation coordinators.

Creation of the following analytical tools will improve understanding of freight systems:

1. **Freight Analysis Framework** (FAF) – The FAF has produced cargo flow maps (based on 1998 data) and projected cargo flow forecast maps with 2020 freight estimates. These maps are helping transportation officials at all levels to focus their attention on freight issues.

2. **Intermodal Transportation Data** – Good data is critical to evidence-based policy and planning and investment decisions. The collection of accurate freight data is an extraordinary challenge. The Bureau of Transportation Statistics (BTS) now manages the TranStats intermodal transportation database (as authorized in TEA-21). BTS also continues to manage the DOT Commodity Flow Survey. In addition, the Department has announced a new Transportation Services Index. This index will track freight and passenger trends.

3. **Intelligent Transportation Systems (ITS) Deployment and Intermodal Freight** – SAFETEA encourages ITS intermodal projects, with the understanding that freight system capacity improvements can be achieved both through infrastructure building and improved IT systems, which facilitate improved freight logistics.

   ITS is a valuable analytical tool because it allows the user/driver/captain to plan a trip based on the most current information available. It also allows the user to make last minute changes, if necessary. For example, before leaving the port with a container, the driver will check the ITS to ascertain that the typical route is still the best route i.e. there are no accidents or construction. Maps on an ITS system are generally more detailed and are easier to read.

DOT anticipates that these provisions included in our SAFETEA proposal, if enacted, will play a vital role in helping to develop a national freight intermodal system. SAFETEA will produce:

- Freight coordination on the state level to help streamline multi-state infrastructure projects;

- Capacity building, not just on the interstate highways, but across all modes of carriage for commercial and military freight;

- Freight-related training programs and awareness training on the state and Metropolitan Planning Organization (MPO) levels;

- Continuation and enhancement of the Freight Analysis Framework;

- Intermodal connector funding, particularly where "last mile" congestion is having an impact on both the local community and the freight carriers;

- Planning on a national level for an enhanced intermodal system rather than for only individual modal providers;

35

- Refinement of the TIFIA program to direct funding to smaller projects and public-private partnerships in order to leverage scarce financial resources; and

- An expanded International Gateways Program that provides planning and development of corridors beyond the current NAFTA border crossings.

In addition to these freight initiatives and important new actions under SAFETEA, DOT is developing a proposal that focuses on much needed marine and intermodal improvements.

B. Future Actions

1. DOT/ MARAD: A Targeted Approach

Given current needs and projected requirements that will be placed on America's national transportation system and its marine component, DOT/MARAD believe that a targeted approach to full integration of a strengthened marine mode into the national intermodal system, is essential. Development of such an approach is now underway. It includes strengthening Federal Government coordination and management, conducting a thorough assessment of MTS needs across the system, and taking specific actions to improve the competitiveness of the U.S. maritime industries. As part of this effort, we will also focus on leveraging funds from Federal, state and local governments, as well as the private sector, to address MTS needs and ensure broad state and local government and private sector input. The ultimate goal is to deliver a marine transportation system that enhances the efficiency, productivity, and capacity of our nation's intermodal transportation system. The better utilization of America's waterways will mitigate the congestion that is otherwise inevitable as overland freight shipments increase.

The objectives of this targeted approach are to:

- Coordinate Federal programs and regulatory activities having an impact on the MTS through leadership provided by the Secretary of Transportation and the Department;

- Strengthen the MTS and its underlying infrastructure through emphasis comparable to that given other modes of transportation;

- Improve intermodal connectivity by improving integration of the marine mode into the national transportation system;

- Explore improvements to marine and intermodal financing directed at the physical landside and waterside infrastructure that also addresses military needs and security such as tax incentives and leveraged public/private financing; and

- Reverse decades of decline in our nation's merchant marine and shipbuilding capabilities through measures to reduce regulatory and tax burdens and improve efficiency and competitiveness.

2. Operation Iraqi Freedom: A Test of Our Deployment Capabilities

OIF has provided the U.S. Government with a unique opportunity to "stress test" our strategic commercial ports and mobilization technologies. The strategic commercial ports and the transportation industry did an outstanding job of supporting the military in OIF with minimal commercial cargo disruptions.

Significant improvements in the transportation system can be made based on lessons learned from OIF. A number of impediments were identified that need to be addressed so future deployments work as well in a more congested transportation system. Based on the lessons learned, MARAD has the following specific recommendations for enhancing our strategic commercial ports and their intermodal capabilities.

a. Strengthen our Commercial Port, Highway, and Rail System as a Strategic Asset

Commercial port operators build and maintain infrastructure based on commercial requirements. There is little excess capacity in the commercial port system for future needs. Port rail infrastructure shortfalls are expected to become more serious in the future as trade grows, with potentially larger military deployments possibly occurring in conflict with seasonal cargo surges. MARAD needs to work further with port operators and DOD to assess the extent of the problem and evaluate ways to enhance strategic commercial port operations to better meet military needs.

b. Facilitate the Development and Effective Use of Port Staging Areas for Strategic Cargo

The one critical infrastructure impediment to effective military deployment at our strategic commercial ports is the availability of port staging areas. Expansion is difficult because competition for waterfront real estate is intense and conflicting uses make it nearly impossible for ports to acquire additional land. This pressure for waterfront real estate will continue.
MARAD must work with the strategic commercial ports and DOD to explore innovative and cost effective ways to address this problem. Solutions may not necessarily be restricted to using DOD or commercial property adjacent to, or close to strategic ports, but should also include technology improvements identified in the rail infrastructure section above. MARAD, the strategic ports, and DOD should collaborate to identify the technologies that will help increase cargo in-transit visibility, cargo throughput, deployment velocity, and other options to reduce military staging area requirements.

c. Capitalize on Advanced Communications Infrastructure Technologies

The communication infrastructure at the strategic commercial ports is sufficient during peacetime but is not robust enough to handle the increased requirements during a major deployment or national emergency. This lack of infrastructure made it difficult for deployment stakeholders to communicate and coordinate cargo operations early in the build-up and mobilization phases of OIF.

The Interoperability Assessment Report (underway) will provide MARAD with specific recommendations for communication infrastructure upgrades. Improvements that have already been identified in the MARAD RRF OIF Report[27] include:

- "MARAD should obtain Defense Messaging System capability to ensure effective message traffic receipt at MARAD Headquarters, and provide written guidelines, standards, requirements, and procedures for MARAD region command centers."

- "MARAD should also investigate ways to expand the Secure Internet Protocol Router Network (SIPRNET) access to MARAD headquarters and regional offices, and investigate the use of SIPRNET-Lite capability on RRF ships."

d. Coordinate Transportation among SDDC, Army/Marine Bases, and the Commercial Carriers

A factor that contributed to the early deployment congestion was a lack of visibility over the arrival of cargo trains and trucks. As the deployment continued, the SDDC learned to hold daily port operations meetings and teleconferences with the Army bases, ports, and the railroads to coordinate cargo flow and provide in-transit visibility. They also learned that communicating the composition of the cargo to be deployed through the ports in *advance of its arrival* greatly enhanced the cargo handling operation.

Detailed deployment planning prior to mobilization was identified as a problem at the NPRN Strategic Port Workshop in September 2001. Additional planning with the industry (port, rail, labor, and truck) will allow the industry to help DOD find ways to further increase efficiency and possibly speed up future deployment.

MARAD together with SDDC and the industry should assess the possible establishment of a Planning Advisory Committee with industry stakeholders. This committee can then be used to: (1) analyze DOD port/intermodal service and resource requirements; (2) identify commercial port and intermodal capacity that may be used to meet DOD requirements; and (3) develop and recommend Concepts of Operations (CONOPS) to meet DOD-approved contingency requirements.

e. Enhance Readiness Training and Provide Compensation

The September 2001 NPRN workshops and the OIF interviews concluded that current port training arrangements were not adequate for actual deployment. These training exercises currently include:

- Port readiness training conducted by the local Port Readiness Committees (PRCs) during port readiness exercises held every other year at the strategic commercial ports;

- MARAD and the American Association of Port Authorities national port readiness workshops; and

---

[27] "The RRF in Operation Iraqi Freedom - Lessons Learned," U.S. Department of Transportation, Maritime Administration, Office of Ship Operations, February 6, 2004.

- DOD (through U.S. Army Forces Command) Sea Emergency Deployment Readiness Exercises (SEDRE).

In addition, strategic commercial ports, terminals, railroads, longshore labor, and trucking companies are not compensated for their mobilization readiness activities. Longshore labor has also expressed concerns about not having a sufficient number of skilled laborers, especially skilled drivers for military equipment during OIF.

Terminals at the strategic commercial ports are subject to National Shipping Authority Service Priority Orders that make these facilities less attractive for commercial lease by introducing an element of business uncertainty in the operation. Assured port access carries a price. Some have suggested that the Federal government provide financial incentives to assist the strategic ports to meet their commitments under this program.

MARAD should assess possible incentives to compensate strategic ports and other deployment stakeholders for peacetime port readiness training. MARAD should also evaluate the possibility of more frequent and comprehensive port outload exercises and expand the exercises to include rail and truck scenarios. In addition, MARAD should coordinate with SDDC to establish a longshore labor training program. The RRF OIF Report concluded that, "MARAD should coordinate with MSC and SDDC to activate and employ RRF ships for routine and special exercises to the greatest extent possible. Active service is the best proving ground for identifying ship equipment shortcomings, needed maintenance and repairs, and required training for crews and reservists...."

C. A National Approach for MTS Enhancement and Growth

A major East Coast container port representative stated that, "The Government needs to realize and base funding decisions on the fact that the nation benefits from port investments." With the mandate to improve military deployment capabilities, national security measures, and freight related economic opportunities, MARAD is in a position to unify the port and maritime community. To accomplish this, MARAD has identified a set of actions that are uniquely suited to address major issues that slow MTS enhancement and growth.

1. Create a National Listing of Operational Port Impediments

Creating a national list of port impediments would help to identify specific impediments and conditions causing congestion in our national port system. This is the first step in solving congestion-causing issues on a systemic level.

2. Develop a Framework of Best Practices to Encourage Short Sea Shipping

Short Sea Shipping is a term used to describe an intermodal waterborne transportation system. It is gaining recognition among states as a critical means of reducing port-related truck and rail traffic congestion that has an impact on the local community. MARAD will work with states, ports, and operators to determine the characteristics that will make short sea shipping successful. These best practices will be published to explain how and where these short sea successes are working. For example, the metropolitan planning authority that includes Bridgeport, Connecticut believes short sea shipping can take 41,000 trucks per year off of I-95.

3. Facilitate New Port Access and Infrastructure Projects

The ports themselves identified several specific issues that can either facilitate or impede new port access and infrastructure projects:

- A port representative stated, "There should be a port or intermodal fund like there is with highways and with airports." The source of this suggested fund was not identified.

- A labor group stated, "Someone is going to have to do something to address unmet funding needs because it is in the State and Federal governments' best interest."

- Several port representatives indicated that their revenue and local funding for infrastructure development was being used for port security requirements and that every local dollar that is moved from infrastructure to security means a loss of ten dollars in infrastructure financing through leveraged loans.

4. Create and Implement a World Class Best Practices Guide For Port Congestion Management

Ports and operators are constantly searching for new and better techniques for freight management. Ports in the United States have told us that they are struggling against an accumulation of empty containers, limited land, conflicting agreements for longshore work hours and several other practices. Experts worldwide have started to address these and other issues such as: solving the truck idling issue; limiting unneeded equipment in the port; and standard planning for major transportation abnormalities such as accidents and weather incidents. New strategies are also developing around concepts such as agile ports, and ports signaling for cargo rather than shippers simultaneously inundating waterfront terminals. However, there is no central forum or publication where these new and developing ideas may be discussed.

5. Improve Road and Rail Services that Have an Impact on Military Deployments and Local Communities

The ports have told MARAD that in many cases the transportation infrastructure is simply not adequate to handle current, moderately growing, or spikes in trade. As trade grows, so will congestion, thus reducing the ability of the intermodal transportation system to efficiently handle normal commercial and emergency military or humanitarian cargoes. Road and rail access to the ports urgently needs development, and cannot be counted on to handle the full brunt of the expected high-end growth in trade. To address these needs, DOT has developed a National Freight Action Plan with MARAD and the Saint Lawrence Seaway Development Corporation as key partners. The plan will seek new ways to improve intermodal connections and consider alternative ways of moving commercial freight to support the nation's growing economy while minimizing related congestion.

6. Develop and Promulgate Best Practices Training for Innovative Port Finance

Several ports indicated the need to address funding issues through innovative practices. To familiarize the ports with new innovative transportation funding programs established by DOT for other transportation modes, MARAD will develop a best practices training session on financing opportunities and how to apply these processes to best meet their needs.

7. Promote Maintenance and New Dredging in the Ports

Lack of attention to port maintenance and improvement dredging is starting to restrict trade and military movements. Some ports are struggling to keep up with newer, deeper draft container vessels which are now calling on the United States. Further, military movements onto some deployment docks are restricted to daylight operation because of channel width and depth restrictions. MARAD recommends that some of the most critical dredging and infrastructure projects be identified for the purpose of bringing attention to the areas that may soon restrict military or significant commercial cargo.

This Page Intentionally Blank

Chapter VI.   Summary and Conclusion

A. Summary:

The Conference Report to accompany the FY 2004 Omnibus Appropriations legislation directed MARAD to report on the performance of the intermodal system with respect to the efficiency of the most congested ports. The Committees requested that MARAD: provide a summary of the performance of the 14 strategic commercial ports during the military force build-up for OIF, compare the most congested ports in terms of operational efficiency; identify the most glaring deficiencies of the intermodal system as a whole as they relate to ports; identify significant intermodal obstacles associated with each port; and provide a summary of future actions that MARAD plans to take to address and improve the throughput of cargo in America's ports.

MARAD wishes to emphasize that while this report is presented by the agency, it is the product of close collaboration with other DOT components, from the development of the data gathering framework to information analysis and presentation. This collaboration underscores how imperative it is to see transportation as a national intermodal system, not as separate unconnected parts. This report also reflects collaboration and input from the scientific community, the private sector, and state and local governments. It proceeds, above all, from an appreciation that our nation's transportation system must always rest on the essential foundation of a solid and sustained public/private-sector partnership.

OIF Deployment: MARAD found that during the OIF deployment, the strategic commercial ports and the transportation industry were able to support the military requirements with minimal commercial cargo disruptions. Military operational deployments require the large-scale use of RO/RO ships, which are capable of carrying a combination of aircraft, wheeled and tracked vehicles, oversize equipment, and containers. Four of the ports – Jacksonville, FL; Beaumont, TX; Corpus Christi, TX; and Charleston, SC carried over 75 percent of the tonnage shipped from the CONUS ports. Occasional congestion problems were resolved within a few days. The impact of a deployment can vary by port and situation; however, there was greater urgency in the four ports that moved most of the volume.

Comparison of Congested Ports: MARAD was unable to provide the requested comparison of the most congested ports in terms of operational efficiency due to a lack of consistent national port efficiency data. Given the diverse characteristics of U.S. ports, comparing port efficiency would require the creation of new methodologies and the collection of data that were not available for this report. To address this issue, MARAD developed an innovative approach to meet the Committees' request by collecting information directly via site visits and a limited number of structured interviews with stakeholders, rather than employing a traditional survey. A list of all questions used for the visits appears in Appendix B. MARAD did not seek to collect information on the deficiencies of port management or labor practices. Rather, the collected information is a snapshot of the current congestion conditions in the U.S. intermodal system and its impact on military deployments.

The MARAD-led DOT intermodal teams focused on two separate operating scenarios of the MTS: normal commercial traffic, and the unique requirements of a military deployment through commercial ports. Port specific information was also gathered from other sources, including DOD, commercial shippers, and previous reports. The following significant concerns were raised for both commercial port operations and military deployments:

- Cargo Volume During Surge
- Staging Area for Cargo
- Landside Access to Ports
- Port Rail Infrastructure
- Waterside Access - Channel and Port Dredging
- Increasing Trade Volumes
- Finance of Infrastructure and Security Improvements
- Highway Signage
- Intermodal Connectivity
- Communications

The additional following concerns were raised for military deployment operations:

- Assured Access to Strategic Ports
- Training of Civilian Personnel to Handle Military Cargoes
- Coordination Among Military Bases, Ports, and Railroads

In the course of its investigation, MARAD learned that several ports are already struggling with intermodal transportation overload, and that infrastructure impediments are not the only factors contributing to port congestion in the United States. While there were a wide variety of themes in response to MARAD's questions, there was much agreement on the urgent congestion and infrastructure issues facing the MTS. About half the ports cited specific congestion that causes infrastructure overload. One fourth of the ports described their infrastructure impediments as "severe." The responses mirror the concerns raised in recent DOT, GAO, and non-government studies on MTS issues.

The issues that ports raised during the site visits have been independently confirmed in other public sector, academic and industry reviews and analyses of the intermodal system. There have been a significant number of surveys and reports completed in the last decade, which indicate that continued enhancement of productivity of the MTS must be a national objective.

Additionally, security is a new major challenge for the intermodal system. The new security imperatives are an everyday challenge for transportation providers, especially at ports. Ports are being called upon to tighten their security and be ready to support military operations when needed, while at the same time moving ever-increasing volumes of commercial traffic. The goal of both industry and the government is to protect the nation's maritime infrastructure from catastrophe, and at the same time, not disrupt the nation's economy by hampering the flow of commerce.

To date, the transportation system and its MTS component have kept pace with the growth of commerce. Even with the significant productivity gains in the freight system, over the past few years, warning signals indicate that a new focus on systemic freight investment is needed.

Future Actions: MARAD analyzed the current challenges to the nation's intermodal freight transportation system and addressed the transportation issues that have an impact on the future of a key component of MTS, our port industry. To avoid dramatic and adverse impacts on our economy and our national defense capabilities, public and private freight transportation stakeholders are already formulating recommendations that if adopted today will guide port transportation system policies for the future. Some of these recommendations include:

- Create a National Freight Policy using the policies and guidelines of ISTEA and TEA-21. This can provide a foundation for real economic and national defense advances for the nation's intermodal transportation system. As the National Chamber Foundation of the U.S. Chamber of Commerce stated in its Study on Trade and Transportation, the National Freight Policy needs to link our nation's transportation industries horizontally to form an integrated intermodal freight system within DOT's structure.

- Develop a proposal for a comprehensive DOT Marine Transportation/Marine Industry initiative. This targeted effort will focus on the waterborne aspect of a National Freight Policy. The proposal will address ways to enhance intermodal coordination under the DOT leadership within the Department while helping to ensure that our maritime transportation system continues to support economic growth and job creation for years to come. It is vital to our ability to meet projected growth and the demands of global economic competition and world trade; secure reliable mobility and force projection for our Armed Forces; and the continued economic strength of our nation and the well-being of its citizens.

- To ensure an intermodal freight network for our future terminals, DOT must develop an approach that maximizes the ability of public and private project sponsors to leverage public capital to improve our transportation systems and eliminate impediments in contracting for intermodal projects.

- In the United States, the development and operation of railroads has long been the responsibility of the private sector. The reliance on railroads by our public transportation network will continue to increase into the future.

- Establish a National Intelligent Freight Network to improve "cargo visibility" within the transportation system/MTS. Such a network will provide benefits to the users of the system and provide a foundation for minimizing freight transport risk in the post 9/11 world. It could provide economic benefits to shippers, carriers, freight forwarders, terminal operators, rail and surface transportation providers, and the public port authorities.

- MARAD should develop partnerships with private industry, including maritime, road and rail constituents to address issues of mutual concern as addressed in this report.

B. Conclusion

Operation Iraqi Freedom's test of the Nation's mobilization capacity highlights the fact that our transportation system must operate in an integrated, intermodal manner if we are to respond quickly to future mobilizations. In addition to the growing volume of cargo moving through our Nation's ports and the increased security challenges throughout the MTS, there are 17 Federal agencies in six cabinet-level departments currently responsible for maritime decision-making. In the past, this has led to a patchwork of inefficient laws, polices, and programs.

That is why President Bush, in his response to the Commission on Oceans Policy, has called for the Department of Transportation to work with other Federal agencies with responsibilities associated with the MTS to improve interagency coordination. This will be accomplished with the elevation of the existing Interagency Committee on the Marine Transportation System (ICMTS) to the cabinet level and using that forum to assess MTS needs, review Federal and non-Federal programs designed to meet those needs, and identify ways to fill any remaining gaps. The result will be a more integrated MTS policy-making structure across the Federal government, which will help us to ensure that we can continue to support our troops when called upon to do so.

Previous reports and studies also point to a need for system-wide investments in the national transportation system with better coordination of expenditures on highways, public mass transit, rail, airports, MTS, and other essential intermodal connectors where they intersect. As DOT/MARAD move to take a more systemic approach to MTS policy development, by better integrating the public and private sectors, as well as local, State, and Federal interests, we must do so as part of a coordinated national transportation policy across all modes. With this approach, we can also identify the intermodal infrastructure investment and public and private partnerships needed to build an integrated freight system that can meet future commercial and national defense requirements.

Despite progress in the 1991 Intermodal Surface Transportation Efficiency Act and the Transportation Equity Act for the 21st Century to improve intermodal connectivity, significant gaps still exist in programs, policies, and funding related to creating and maintaining an intermodal system which functions as the kind of seamless system we need to compete in the global economy. In response, the Administration has proposed a series of freight related initiatives in the Safe, Accountable, Flexible, and Efficient Transportation Equity Act of 2003. These include dedicated funding for intermodal connectors between major highways and ports or rail facilities, up to $15 billion in private activity bonds to fund highway and intermodal projects, and the creation of a freight coordinator in each state to ensure that freight-related projects get sufficient attention in state and regional planning processes.

Given current needs and projected requirements that will be placed on America's national transportation system and its essential marine mode component, DOT/MARAD believe that comprehensive marine transportation system improvements, which include the full integration of a strengthened marine mode into the national intermodal system, are essential. At the direction of the President, the Administration is exploring ways of strengthening Federal Government coordination and management of the Marine Transportation/Maritime Industry.

This targeted approach is expected to include strengthening Federal Government coordination and management, conducting a thorough assessment of MTS needs across the system, and the removal of non-market obstacles that impede development of U.S. maritime industries. As part of this effort, DOT/MARAD will also focus on leveraging funds from Federal, state and local governments, as well as the private sector, to address MTS needs and ensure broad state and local government and private sector input. The ultimate goal is to deliver a marine transportation system that enhances the efficiency, productivity, and capacity of our nation's intermodal transportation system. The better utilization of America's waterways will mitigate the congestion that is otherwise inevitable as overland freight shipments increase.

Supplementing SAFETEA, which is now awaiting action by the Congress, the DOT/MARAD efforts will help meet the challenges of the future; especially much needed infrastructure repair and replacement. Progress toward the goal will require a sustained commitment from government and private sector leaders alike. However, the successful implementation of these much-needed improvements will generate significant economic activity, increase tax revenues, and create American jobs, both while these projects are underway and well into the future.

This Page Intentionally Blank

Appendix A. National Port Readiness Network

Military Functions—Strategic Ports for Military Deployment—the National Port Readiness Network

MARAD chairs the National Port Readiness Network (NPRN) which promotes the readiness of the fourteen commercial strategic ports and three continental U.S. military ports.[28] The NPRN mission is to support the secure movement of military forces through U.S. strategic ports. These ports support deployment of military surge and sustainment cargo. In peacetime, MARAD works closely with DOD and the 14 U.S. strategic commercial ports to ensure the readiness of these ports and their intermodal infrastructure to accept and process military deployments.

The 14 Strategic Ports

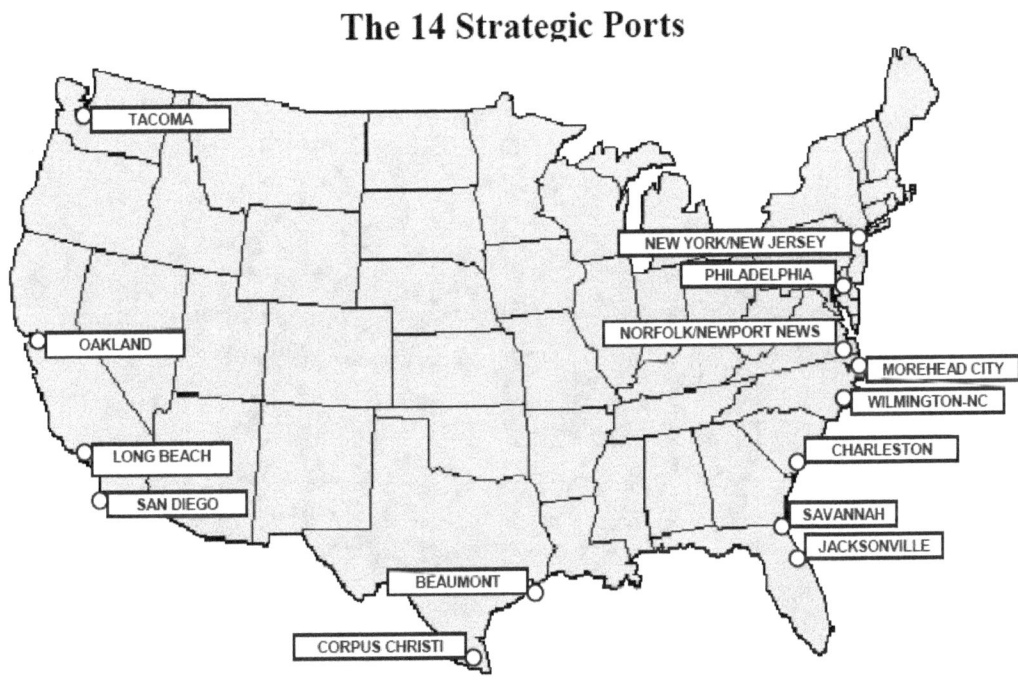

DOT, through MARAD, is responsible for ensuring DOD's priority for use of commercial ports, terminals, and related intermodal facilities during deployments or other defense emergencies. Pursuant to the Defense Production Act of 1950 (DPA), MARAD can require strategic commercial ports to provide priority use of their facilities and services to DOD ahead of their normal commercial contractual obligations.

Based on DOD deployment requirements, MARAD issues Port Planning Orders (PPOs) to the strategic commercial ports in accordance with Title 46 CFR, Part 340. These PPOs are non-binding planning arrangements that identify port facilities and services that may be needed by DOD in the event of a deployment or other defense emergency.

---

[28] Military Ocean Terminal Sunny Point, NC; Concord Naval Weapons Station, CA; and Port Hadlock, WA.

MARAD also has in place standby Federal Port Controller (FPC) service agreements with key executives at the strategic ports. Each FPC is responsible for controlling the utilization of port facilities, equipment, and services. MARAD and DOD work closely with the FPCs to prioritize military cargo movements to expedite the dispatch of military cargo while minimizing congestion and disruption to commercial activities.

The organization does its work through a Steering Group, a Working Group, and local Port Readiness Committees (PRCs). The PRCs provide the means for coordinating port readiness planning in peacetime, provide training through exercises, and coordinate port operations and security during a deployment or other military activity.[29]

National Port Readiness Network Organization

Interagency Agreement	Levels of Coordination	Responsibilities
MARAD (Chair) TRANSCOM SDDC MSC USACE USCG FORSCOM TSA NORTHCOM	Steering Group	Sets policy direction and priorities
	Working Group	Implements policies and priorities
	Local Port Readiness Committee	Execution of Coordinates peacetime preparation & port operations & security

To ensure that MARAD was in a position to coordinate final planning for the OIF deployment with little to no disruption to our commercial systems, MARAD worked with the Port Readiness Committees. MARAD validated security clearances, tested port secure communications equipment, held a NPRN working group meeting to review final plans, and began frequent communications with MSC and the SDDC. In the early stages of the deployment, MARAD liaison officers were sent to MSC and SDDC installations, and MARAD Region port personnel, together with Merchant Marine Reservists (MMRs), were positioned at the strategic commercial ports during loadouts. MARAD

---

[29] This organization was created by a Memorandum of Understanding and comprises nine Federal agencies: Maritime Administration (MARAD), U.S. Coast Guard (USCG), U.S. Transportation Command (USTRANSCOM), U.S. Northern Command (USNORTHCOM), Transportation Security Administration (TSA), U.S. Army Corps of Engineers (USACE), U.S. Army Forces Command (FORSCOM), Surface Deployment and Distribution Command (SDDC, formerly the Military Traffic Management Command), and the Military Sealift Command (MSC).

activated its headquarters command operations center in the DOT Crisis Management Center. Forty MARAD Ready Reserve Force (RRF) vessels were utilized during OIF.[30]

---

[30] The RRF in Operation Iraqi Freedom, Lessons Learned. Office of Ship Operations, Maritime Administration, DOT. February 6, 2004.

This Page Intentionally Blank

Appendix B. Interview Questions for the Port Intermodal Congestion Study

Interviews were conducted with various port officials at the 23 ports around the country to respond to the congressional direction to assess:

> "..The overall performance of the intermodal system with respect to the efficiency of the most congested ports. Within this report, particular emphasis should be placed on the summarizing the performance of the 14 strategic ports during the military force build up for Operation Iraqi Freedom and on identifying the most glaring deficiencies of the intermodal system as a whole."[31]

It was emphasized in the discussions with the port officials that the interviews were an information gathering exercise requested by Congress, and not a competition for Federal port funds. The report did not seek to collect information on the deficiencies of port management or labor practices, but rather for a snapshot of the current congestion conditions in the United States intermodal system and their impact on military deployments. The interview topic questions follow:

QUESTIONS FOR ALL PORTS

1. How does your port forecast and plan for commercial cargo growth? Do you contract for cargo forecasts, if so, what is the forecast planning horizon?
2. By way of comparison and contrast to your commercial planning efforts, how do you work with your military partners to plan for military movements through your port? Please describe the determination of the planning horizon and forecast levels of military cargo?
3. International trade is expected to double by 2020. Will this doubling of trade affect your port operations? Will a doubling of trade affect military deployments through your port?
4. Does your port have adequate intermodal access to all port facilities?
5. Do you depend on a single delivery mode (road or rail) which causes efficiency or congestion problems?
6. Describe additional modal access your port may need, based on commercial and military requirements.
7. What intermodal factors cause congestion at your port?
8. Are there additional terminals, inland port facilities or staging areas that can be accessed if port demand increases dramatically?
9. When port congestion occurs, how does this affect port activities, for inbound and outbound cargo?
10. What key elements to increase efficiency are outside the control of your port?
11. What initiatives do you have planned to increase efficiency at your port?
12. Are there Federal or State initiatives to help increase efficiency your port?
13. Would short sea shipping (inter coastal service) enhance productivity and efficiency at your port?
14. Are current security requirements impacting port efficiency?
15. Do you anticipate any infrastructure funding issues?
16. Do you have any recommendations or suggestions for the study team?

---

[31] U.S. House of Representatives, Conference Committee on Appropriations, "Report 108-243, Departments of Transportation and Treasury and Independent Agencies Appropriations Bill, FY 2004" (Washington, DC, July 30, 2003), p. 132.

The following questions were only asked of officials at ports that handled OIF cargo.

Operation Iraqi Freedom Ports

1. How did the buildup for Operation Iraqi Freedom (OIF) (January - April 2003) impact your normal port activities? Congestion?
2. Were there training issues related to handling OIF cargo?
3. Were port planning orders adequate for handling OIF cargo?
4. Did handling OIF cargo negatively impact any commercial customers? If so, how? Were there any commercial vessel disruptions or delays and how did they affect operations? Are you aware of any rail or commercial truck issues?
5. If your port became more congested as a result of OIF, what steps and initiatives could have been taken to relieve this congestion?
6. Did you have a shortage of land, labor or equipment (yard hustlers, container cranes, etc.) for OIF requirements?
7. Was there adequate communication and coordination among deployment organizations during OIF buildup and load out? (point of contact for communications and coordination)
8. Was security adequate for military cargo movements and for your normal operation during the buildup to OIF? If not, why not?
9. Was the port adequately compensated in a timely manner by the military for its use of facilities and services during the buildup to OIF?
10. Do you have any suggestions that could enhance military deployments while maintaining normal commercial activities at your port?

MARAD inadvertently did not coordinate these questions with the Office of Management and Budget, as required under the Paperwork Reduction Act (PRA.). Action is being taken to ensure future compliance with the PRA. However, the information collected was not compromised.

Appendix C. Summary and Analysis of Prior Government and Industry Reports and Surveys.

The issues that ports raised with MARAD during the site visits have been independently confirmed in other public sector, academic and industry reviews and analyses of the intermodal system. There have been a significant number of surveys and reports completed in the last decade that indicate that continued enhancement of productivity of the MTS must be a national objective. To date, the transportation system and its MTS component have kept pace with the growth of commerce. Productivity gains have been realized through successful supply chain management information technologies, private sector capital investment, public investment, rationalization and streamlining in the freight carriage sector and some policy adjustments where governmental institutions have begun to focus on emerging freight capacity issues. Even with the significant productivity gains in the freight system, recent warning signals indicate that a new focus on systemic freight investment is needed. It cannot be assumed that multiple institutions can optimize continued responsiveness of a system under pressure.[32]

A. Summaries of the 2003 Intermodal and 2004 Infrastructure Reports

The table below identifies and correlates the crossover issues and terminology used in each of the reports. For example, the Port Efficiency Report discusses information systems whereas the 2003 Intermodal Report limits discussion of information systems to road access conditions. The 2004 Infrastructure Report refers to information systems as an infrastructure support system.

Terminology by Report		
Port Performance and Intermodal Efficiency Report	Intermodal Report	2004 Infrastructure Report
Intermodal Connectivity	Key System Elements by Mode	Interface
	Attributes with high percentages of Unacceptable Conditions	Road/Rail Access to ports
Information Systems	Road Access Conditions, only	Support: Infrastructure (e.g. tagging, tracking, etc.) Vessel/Weather tracking systems Maritime Security Enhancements
Labor	N/A	Support: Human Resources
Terminal Productivity	Road, Rail, Water Access Conditions	Landside: Terminal Capacity (efficiency and throughput)
Intermodal Improvements	Road, Rail, Water Access Conditions	Identified specific projects at specific ports

---

[32] The Marine Transportation System and the Federal Role, Committee for a Study of the Federal Role in the Marine Transportation System, Measuring Performance, Targeting Improvement, TRANSPORTATION RESEARCH BOARD OF THE NATIONAL ACADEMIES, Transportation Research Board, Washington, D.C., 2004, Executive Summary., p. ES 3-4.

The two executive summaries that follow are exact copies of the executive summaries in the reports listed as items one and two.

1. Intermodal Access to U.S. Ports Report on the 2002-2003 Survey Findings, Prepared for U.S. Maritime Administration, U.S. Department of Transportation, by A. Strauss-Weider, Inc., January 2004

Executive Summary

The 2002-2003 Intermodal Access Survey is the second annual assessment of conditions on the connections that serve our nation's ports. Expanding on the first survey, which covered deepwater port authorities in 2001, the 2002-2003 survey was distributed to a broader section of the nation's marine transportation system – deepwater and river port authorities, along with private sector terminal operators. Taken together, the 2002-2003 survey responses represent one of the most complete pictures of current conditions on the road, rail and water access connections to our nation's ports.

During the first survey, the nation was in a recession. In 2002, the U.S. and world economies began moving into recovery, and the amount of international containerized cargo grew substantially. Between 2001 and 2002, the number of twenty-foot equivalent containers or TEUs handled by U.S. ports grew by almost 2 million units, or 6 percent. The nation's ports handled 32.4 million TEUs in 2002. However, roadway congestion continued and the number of rail freight issues increased. The average size of world's fleet of container vessels also grew. While some key access projects were completed, many others are still in either the construction or planning stages.

The report on the 2001 Intermodal Access Conditions Survey noted that:

> "The current state of the intermodal access system for U.S. ports is generally acceptable for handling the existing volumes of cargo flows. However, 'acceptable' is a different condition than 'optimal.' Acceptable means that ports, freight transportation providers and shippers can work around problems and can tolerate a certain amount of delay and costs. Acceptable conditions can quickly become unacceptable as cargo volumes increase in the future or if a segment of the system becomes unusable."[33]

It is, therefore; perhaps not surprising that conditions on the nation's intermodal access system became more unacceptable in 2002/2003. Areas of growing concern include:

- Flow conditions on local roads: Thirty-one percent of deepwater port authorities and 37 percent of the deepwater terminal operators indicated unacceptable flow conditions on the local roads that connect their maritime facilities to the nation. Turning lanes and radii on local roads were also of increasing concern.

---

[33] Intermodal Access to U.S. Ports Report on Survey Findings, Prepared for U.S. Maritime Administration, U.S. Department of Transportation, by A. Strauss-Weider, Inc., August 2002, p.18

- Flow conditions on state and interstate roads: Thirty percent of the deepwater port authorities reported unacceptable flow conditions on these roadways, compared with 20 percent in 2001. Twenty-eight percent of the terminal operators reported similar concerns.

- Port-specific signage on local, state and interstate roads: Deepwater port authority reports of unacceptable conditions regarding port-specific signage on state and interstate roads grew from 13 percent in 2001 to 34 percent in 2002. Reports of unacceptable signage conditions on local roads grew from 18 percent to 31 percent.

- Rail freight access: The percentage of deepwater port authorities indicating unacceptable conditions regarding the availability of on-dock rail facilities grew from 8 percent in 2001 to 26 percent in 2002. The deepwater ports reported higher rates of unacceptable conditions regarding the number of rail spurs and tracks serving and within their ports, and on rail line haul moves.

- Sufficient channel depths at deepwater ports: The percentage of deepwater port authorities reporting unacceptable Federal channel depth conditions rose from 26 percent in 2001 to 34 percent in 2002. Nearly 30 percent of the terminal operators expressed similar concerns. The percent of the top 15 deepwater container ports reporting unacceptable channel depth conditions doubled.

The results of investments and collaborative efforts were also evident. Improvements in conditions were reported by the nation's top 15 deepwater container ports in terms of roadways and at-grade rail crossings within their facilities. Aids to navigation posted consistently high ratings, and environmental issues showed improvement.

The responses to the 2002-2003 survey point to the need to complete planned investments in the intermodal access system and re-enforce the criticality of ensuring continued national focus on all elements of the marine transportation system.

2. Marine Transportation System National Infrastructure Needs Assessment: Vol. I – Final Report, Prepared for the United States Department of Transportation, Washington DC, February 2, 2004. [34]

Executive Summary

"… the Port was so alarmed at the loss in tonnage that a study was commissioned in 1951 to discover the causes. This study noted that landside traffic congestion, inadequate warehouses…, and inadequate truck access made it easier for other ports to grab the business."[35]

---

[34] Prepared by Science Applications International Corporation and Mercator Transport Group, LLC., February 2, 2004.

[35] "Aging Gracelessly - The Slow Decline of the Port", *Bay Crossings*, author Guy Span, http://www.baycrossings.com/Archives/2003/01_February/aging_gracelessly_-_the_slow_decline_of_the_port.htm.

Author Guy Span explains the decline from prominence of what was once one of the country's premier ports, the Port of San Francisco. Span describes how, when container shipping was invented, the port did not modernize to accommodate container traffic and "San Francisco's already obsolete finger piers became practically useless for maritime cargo." Today San Francisco is a minor port and most goods must move into and out of the city through other, less direct routes.

In this case, the majority of the shipping business moved to other deepwater ports on the U.S. West Coast and Northwest. In our current multi-national trade environment, the choices available to shippers and shipping lines extend beyond U.S. ports. The decisions we make as a nation for the Marine Transportation System will go a long way in determining the level of service and efficiency that the system will provide to this country.

The recent *MTSNAC Report and Recommendations to the Secretary of Transportation Regarding Marine Transportation Infrastructure*[36] recommended to the Secretary the rationale, guiding principles, and recommended strategies for MTS infrastructure investments. The MTSNAC report identified MTS priorities in the areas of security, infrastructure, information technology, research & development, and human resources.

The basic tenet that justifies a public interest in improving the intermodal transportation system is that the MTS is critical to the U.S. economy and that any failure within the MTS to meet the needs of the economy in terms of capacity or competitiveness will have adverse consequences that outweigh the investment required to meet those needs.

As a complement to MTSNAC report, the Maritime Administrator contracted with a team of experienced transportation professionals from Science Applications International Corporation (SAIC) and Mercator Transport Group (MTG) to conduct a quick response national survey to clarify further the nature of MTS infrastructure needs as viewed by the major stakeholders that use and operate MTS resources. This study, conducted over a 90-day period, used interviews, surveys, teleconferences, and focus groups with a representative set of stakeholders in various regions. These stakeholders include port authorities, terminal operators, shipping lines, marine exchanges, regional port associations, and regional MTS entities. In addition, past studies of infrastructure needs were reviewed. In regions where local or regional MTS entities exist, some had already developed a composite list of infrastructure needs for the region. In other regions, needs of individual seaports and terminals had been identified but had not yet been expressed at the regional level.

For each region, individual projects were grouped and evaluated by type to evaluate potential deficiencies in the system. Rather than concentrate on individual ports or projects within those ports, MTS regions were assessed as a whole, evaluating overall capacity, efficiency, and impact. Types of projects were identified that would help meet regional deficiencies.

---

[36] Prepared by the Marine Transportation System National Advisory Council, "Recommendations for Investment in Our Nation's Marine Transportation System as Part of a Coherent, Coordinated, and Comprehensive Intermodal Transportion Policy"; A Report to the Secretary, November 12, 2003.

Assessment Framework

High-level needs were organized into four categories, illustrated below, representing the basic components of the MTS: Waterside, Port-Terminal, Landside, and Support, representing infrastructure that cuts across multiple categories.

Waterside	Interface (Port/Terminal)	Landside	Support
Dredging	Capacity	Intermodal Connectors	Maritime Security
Navigation Aids	Handling	At-grade crossings	Cargo Tracking
Locks & Dams	Inspection	Rail yards	"Info-structure"
Technology/Shipbuilding	Agile Port Technology	Inland ports	Human Resources
Short Sea Shipping		Dedicated Lanes	

The major goal of this effort was to identify necessary MTS infrastructure improvements and how these improvement projects contribute to the national interest. The framework used for this report was developed to evaluate proposed improvements and U.S. Government investments to the MTS in terms of their contribution to the following strategic goals:

- Allowing the MTS to meet projected capacity requirements
- Improving the efficiency and competitiveness of the MTS
- Reducing the quality of life impacts of the MTS

Each proposed area of improvement was evaluated on its potential contribution to each of these strategic goals.

MTS Infrastructure Needs

Infrastructure improvements common across all MTS regions are listed together in the figure below; infrastructure improvements associated with specific regions are shown with their respective regions. Note that several of these infrastructure improvements apply to deepwater harbors, some to the inland waterways system and others to all aspects of the MTS. Table 1, at the end of this document, shows the relationships to the national strategic goals for the common MTS infrastructure needs.

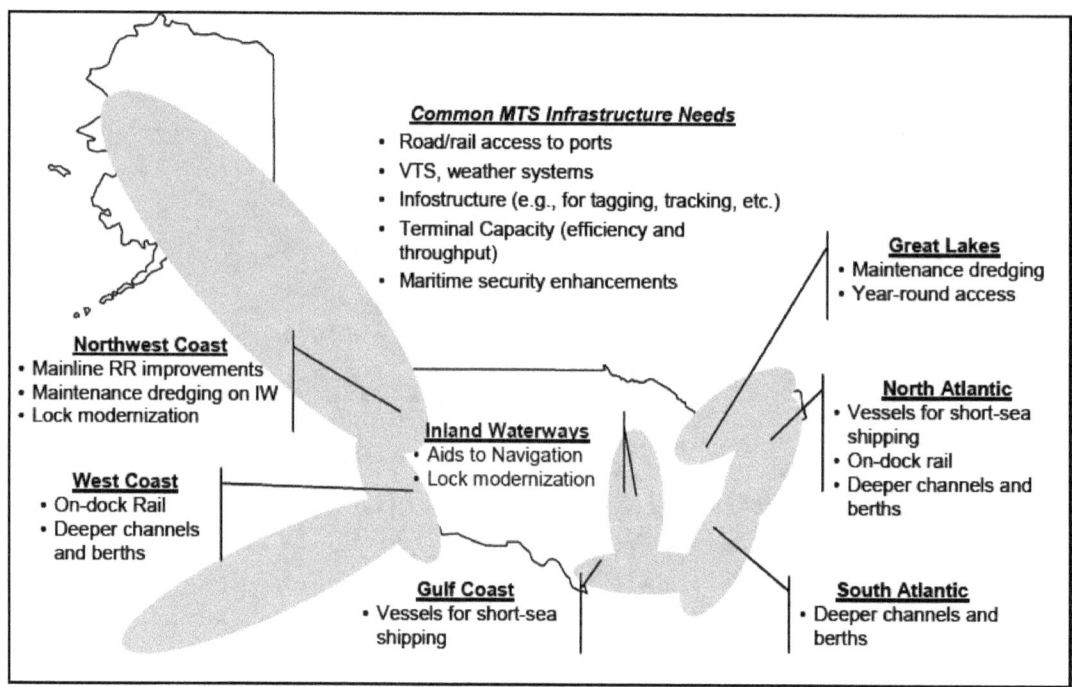

Common MTS Infrastructure Needs
- Road/rail access to ports
- VTS, weather systems
- Infostructure (e.g., for tagging, tracking, etc.)
- Terminal Capacity (efficiency and throughput)
- Maritime security enhancements

Great Lakes
- Maintenance dredging
- Year-round access

North Atlantic
- Vessels for short-sea shipping
- On-dock rail
- Deeper channels and berths

Northwest Coast
- Mainline RR improvements
- Maintenance dredging on IW
- Lock modernization

Inland Waterways
- Aids to Navigation
- Lock modernization

West Coast
- On-dock Rail
- Deeper channels and berths

Gulf Coast
- Vessels for short-sea shipping

South Atlantic
- Deeper channels and berths

Role of Federal Financing

With the exception of the waterways themselves, a majority of the infrastructure within the MTS is privately owned and controlled. However, the intermodal system as a whole is a critical part of the national economy and Federal, state, and local governments have a vested interest in ensuring that it continues to operate in a safe and efficient manner.

This does not mean, however, that all investments in the MTS benefit national strategic goals or that the Federal Government should fund or provide investment incentives for all projects. Ports and intermodal companies within the U.S compete to capture cargo volume. Their motivation and justification to invest in infrastructure improvements may be driven less by the goal of improving the MTS as a whole than by business needs to optimize their portions of it to maintain or gain market share relative to other facilities or other segments of the nation's transportation system.

Funding for MTS infrastructure improvement can come from government sources (Federal, state, local, regional entities), quasi-public sources (e.g., port authorities), and private sector sources. Where public benefit is evident, direct government funding may be appropriate or, alternatively, public/private partnerships through which favorable loan terms and grants are made available to support investments needed to realize the public benefit.

Potential types of Federal Government assistance that can ensure that necessary improvement to the MTS will proceed include:

Direct Federal Funding: For the portions of the MTS that are clearly the domain of government responsibility, such as ocean and in-land waterways, locks, and channels, there is a clear need for direct Federal funding to support infrastructure improvements.

Federal Financial Assistance: Aside from direct Federal funding, there are a number of methods for the Federal Government to provide assistance to private industry to facilitate the improvement of transportation infrastructure. They can include loan guarantees, cost sharing, tax incentives for investment, plus a number of other "innovative" financing methods. These methods of assistance can be attractive for a number of reasons. First, the financing of projects that are pursued using these methods remains primarily under the control of private industry. This helps ensure that project business cases are fundamentally sound and that the projects will be executed with tight controls on costs and schedules. Second, these types of financing schemes maximize the value of the Federal investment. There are many types of infrastructure improvement projects that are not pursued by industry because there is too much risk involved or the return on investment in not quite large enough. Federal assistance can help "push" these projects over the threshold where they are attractive enough to the private companies to warrant investment, without requiring full governmental funding.

Federal Contributions to Business Environment: Besides the various types of financial support that might be provided, there are other legislative paths that the Government can take to facilitate the improvement of the MTS infrastructure. These paths involve the improvement of the business environment in which private companies make decisions on these investments. Primarily, such legislation would involve the streamlining of the environmental approval process, modification of land use laws and regulations, or modification of existing laws that place restrictions on development.

Path to Legislation

In order for of large-scale legislation driving MTS infrastructure improvement to proceed, there are several steps that must take place to ensure that: Federal involvement is properly placed; that such investment is provided in an appropriate manner to important projects; and the return on these investment meet expectations. These steps include:

Development of Metrics for Evaluation of Investments: Although Federal government investments can be justified in an overall sense by the importance of the MTS, there is a definite need for the development of metrics to analyze the potential return on investment of various projects and financing schemes. These metrics must be developed so that different investment opportunities and types of financing can be evaluated and compared, resulting in the greatest return on investment.

Framework for Competitive Selection of Infrastructure Projects: In many cases, the infrastructure improvements needed to maintain U.S. economic competitiveness can take many forms. For instance, if it is determined that there is a need for increased deepwater terminal capacity on the West Coast; there are multiple ports at which this capacity could be provided. It would not make sense to provide deepwater channels at all ports because there would then be significant over-capacity. The Federal Government needs a framework to compare proposals submitted by different entities for infrastructure improvement. This framework must be capable of using the metrics developed for determining which project provides the greatest return on investment.

Detailed Analysis of Infrastructure Needs to Support Strategic Goals: The MTSNAC Report to the Secretary and this MTS National Infrastructure Needs Assessment lay out the basic needs for infrastructure improvement and related investments and funding. In most cases, these infrastructure needs can be meet in multiple ways, ranging from different geographic locations to different technologies to separate designs. Each of these options for meeting national MTS needs has different costs and benefits that accrue to different stakeholders. More detailed analysis of these needs and the alternatives for meeting them is required to support decision-making. These detailed analyses should be based upon the evaluation metrics and selection framework described above.

B. Analysis of Recent MARAD Intermodal Access Surveys

Between 2001-2003, MARAD conducted intermodal access surveys of U.S. ports. For these studies, MARAD sent closed-end questionnaires to numerous deepwater and inland ports. The first report, *"Intermodal Access to U.S. Ports Report on the 2002-2003 Survey Findings"* (2003 Intermodal Report) ranked pre-selected modal impediments of the MTS. The second report, *"Marine Transportation System National Infrastructure Needs Assessment: Vol. I – Final Report"* (2004 Infrastructure Report) arranged its questionnaire by four functional areas: Waterside, Freight Transfer or Terminal, Landside and Overall Support. Twenty-two of the key ports analyzed in this Port Efficiency Report to Congress were also included in the above-mentioned MARAD reports. Although the MARAD intermodal surveys were conducted independently of this report, there are common elements in the results and findings of the intermodal studies that are relevant for this report. [37]

The 2003 Intermodal Report particularly confirms and highlights the findings of the DOT Intermodal team port visits concerning obstacles in the efficient handling of commercial freight. In the 2003 Intermodal Report, ports rated key system elements and other system attributes with a high level of below-average conditions by transportation mode on a descending scale of 1 – 5. To simplify the presentation of the 2003 Intermodal Report findings, MARAD grouped the survey results into above-average for ratings of 1 and 2, average for ratings of 3 and below-average for ratings of 4 and 5. "A rating of average means that ports, freight transportation providers and shippers can work around problems and can tolerate a certain amount of delay and costs. Average conditions can quickly become below average as cargo volumes increase in the future or if a segment of the system becomes unusable."[38] Since this Port Efficiency Report to Congress discusses both defense and commercial issues, the findings of the 2003 Intermodal Report are indicated separately for the Strategic and Non-Strategic Ports.

---

[37] Each report uses different terminology to refer to similar issues. Differences in terminology and a summary of the two MARAD intermodal survey reports are provided in Appendix C.

[38] Intermodal Access to U.S. Ports Report on Survey Findings, August 2002, p. i.

Table 1

		Strategic Ports	Non-Strategic Ports
Percent of Ports Reporting Below Average Flow Conditions on Key System Elements			
Roads	Within Ports	8%	25%
	Local Access	58%	27%
	State & Interstate	45%	30%
Rail	Line Haul Moves	45%	33%
	Shared Rights of way with		
	Passenger Traffic	50%	30%
Water	Sufficient Depth in Federal Channels	42%	40%
	Sufficient Depth in Private Channels and at Berths	50%	38%

The 2003 Intermodal Report found flow conditions on key system elements to be a consistent impediment to port efficiency. When analyzed for the 22 key ports as a whole, 33 percent stated that flow conditions on the road were below average, while rail and water key system elements were found to be below average by 42.5 percent and 6 percent, of the deepwater ports, respectively.[39] Strategic ports fared worse than non-strategic ports in flow conditions in all categories except roads within the ports. Landside access to ports via all modes is one of the crosscutting issues with major ripple effects identified in all three reports. For example, rail congestion on at-grade crossings can impede truck traffic on local access roads and delay the shipment of goods to the customer. To minimize the disruption of service, terminal operators may pay for overtime labor and carriers may delay the ship's departure. Both of these alternatives are very expensive and cannot be sustained as a standard operating procedure. Similar problems and repercussions were identified for road and water access to ports.

The 2004 Infrastructure Report specifically named rail and road access to ports, on-dock railroad access, increased terminal capacity, and increased water depth at major ports as five of the nation's 10 most pressing national MTS priorities. Rail and road access and increased water depth are named as key system elements in the 2003 Intermodal Report, while on-dock rail access and increased terminal capacity are cited as other system attributes with a high percentage of below-average conditions:

---

[39] IBID

Table 2

		Strategic Ports	Non Strategic Ports
Percent of Ports Reporting a High Percentage of Below-Average Conditions for Other System Attributes at Strategic and Other Key Container Ports			
ROADS	Number of turning lanes on local roads	33%	30%
	Turning radii on local roads	50%	33%
	Traffic flow at at-grade rail crossings within ports	42%	33%
	Traffic flow at at-grade rail crossings on local roads	58%	27%
	Signage in port	18%	17%
	Signage on local roads	33%	18%
	Signage on Interstate and State roads	50%	18%
RAIL	Conditions at at-grade crossings (signals & roadbeds)	25%	25%
	Availability of on-dock rail terminals	42%	56%
	Availability of near-dock rail terminals	42%	45%
	No of spurs & tracks serving port	36%	9%
	Number of spurs & tracks within the port	25%	40%
	Cost & travel time associated with moving cargo between port & railheads	33%	27%
WATER	Maintenance dredging of Federal Channels	9%	30%
	Maintenance dredging of private terminals/berths	22%	11%
	Capital Improvements to terminals/berths – private channels berths	33%	33%

Key Issues: Signage

While all three modes (road, rail, and water) experience congestion and traffic flow problems, most containers enter or leave the port by truck. Below-average signage is more prevalent at strategic ports than non-strategic ports. One of the fastest and least expensive means of addressing highway traffic flow problems at the ports is to improve the signage. The 2003 Intermodal Report evaluated signage in three separate areas: interstate and state roads, local roads, and roads within the port. Signage on interstate and state roads was ranked as one of the three worst highway traffic impediments by half of the strategic ports.[40] One-third of the strategic ports found signage on local access roads to be below-average while signage within the ports was rated significantly better at an 18 percent below average level. By comparison, 18 percent of the non-strategic ports ranked signage on interstate, state and local roads as unacceptable. The ramifications of poor signage include more unproductive time spent on the road, increased fuel consumption, and more pollution – all factors that increase the cost of shipping. While better signage will not eliminate traffic congestion, in our analysis, it could provide an effective short-term solution to reduce some highway congestion and

---

[40] Both signage and turning radii on local roads were rated at 50 percent below average levels by the strategic ports. Key system elements at at-grade rail crossings ranked highest with 58 percent of the strategic ports citing unacceptable conditions.

improve safety. It is readily available to all drivers, does not require specialized knowledge of the port, does not require a change or delay to existing traffic patterns, and can be accomplished quickly and inexpensively.

Key Issues: Depth and Dredging

More importantly, the depth at Federal channels was rated below average by 42 percent of the strategic ports. Fully 50 percent of the strategic ports also rated the depth at private channels and berths as below average. Conditions at non-strategic ports were ranked better by 2 and 12 percent, respectively. Maintenance dredging of Federal channels was ranked below average by 9 percent of the strategic ports and 30 percent of the non-strategic ports. Both the strategic and non-strategic ports ranked capital improvements equally unfavorably.

Below-average depths at our deepwater ports have the potential to have a dramatic negative impact on shipping in the United States. As the larger containerships currently being built enter into service over the next four to five years, the scope of the problem could widen to affect even more deepwater ports. Insufficient depth hinders a ship's ability to use the most efficient port, based on cost and/or location. Potentially, insufficient depth and dredging of all our deepwater ports can cause overcrowding at the deepest ports while shallower ports are underutilized. The result is increasing congestion and worsening conditions of key system elements at our busiest and deepest ports that, by their very location have the least room to expand. The 2004 Infrastructure Report's evaluation of depth, including dredging, confirmed this finding when it stated, "Lack of adequate deepwater capacity could result in newest generation container ships making primary calls at foreign ports. U.S. ports would then either be served after ships have been partially discharged abroad or by feeder. This would result in added time/cost to inter-regional shipments and could reduce the overall efficiency of import/export shipping to the rest of the U.S."

Key Issues: Communications

Communications, especially information technology systems, has only recently begun to be recognized as a potential tool that can be used to significantly improve the MTS. In the past five years, only one study, which was funded by the DOT's Office of Intermodalism, and the Federal Highway Administration, evaluated the state of the information technology systems in the MTS.[41] Most studies, including the 2004 Infrastructure Report, still refer to communications and information technology systems as a support function. The 2003 Intermodal Report mentions several technology issues in the road access section of their questionnaire to ports but they are not discussed in the body of the report. The following table shows the findings of the 2003 Intermodal Report for the 22 deepwater ports that are common to all three studies. Congress has also recognized that communications are an important concern. The FY 2004 Appropriation Conference Committee has requested MARAD to issue a separate report entitled *The Interoperability of Information Resources Among Strategic Ports (Interoperability Report)*.

---

[41] Cambridge Systematics Inc., Challenges and Opportunities for an ITS/Intermodal Freight Program prepared for U.S. Department of Transportation, ITS Joint Program Office, February 1999.

Table 3

Percent of Ports Reporting Below Average Communications Issues that Effect Flow Conditions on Roads Serving Deepwater Ports	
Issue	
Electronic tolls or Vehicle ID	
In Port	33%
Access Roads	38%
State/Interstate Roads	13%
Radio Transmission of Local Traffic Conditions	
In Port	18%
Access Roads	26%
State/Interstate Roads	22%
Web Based Traffic Information	
In Port	47%
Access Roads	50%
State/Interstate Roads	36%
Paperless Gates – in port only	71%

The U.S. maritime industry and its intermodal partners currently have a disparate communications system that is typically user or mode specific. It lacks horizontal interface with most of the other entities involved in the shipping process, especially State and Federal government agencies, according to the preliminary findings of the "Interoperability Report." Communications between government agencies frequently depend on personal contacts and networks over non-secure systems.

The current trends toward globalization and just-in-time shipments, as well as the development of a short sea-shipping program, demand state of the art communication systems. These systems must be simple to use, minimize the time involved in completing numerous forms, and interface with many industry participants if they are to speed up cargo movement to the greatest extent possible. The technology is already available but lacks a standard protocol that meets several needs simultaneously and would require a substantial investment at the end-user level. Addressing the communications issues simultaneously with infrastructure, safety, and security needs has the potential to reduce congestion and pollution as well as some human capital and customer service concerns.

Together, the three reports identify many of the same Marine Transportation System issues and serve to reinforce each other by using different approaches to the same issues. The number of common issues in all three reports emphasizes the level of broad-based concerns and supports the suggestion made in several earlier reports: comprehensive Federal planning for a national Marine Transportation System is needed and should be implemented as soon as possible. Because there are so many generic issues accompanied by specific priorities and projects identified in the reports, only a few of the more serious ones were discussed in detail for this report. Appendix C is also based on the 2003 Intermodal Report and ranks port conditions by modes that were not mentioned in the previous tables. Most of them are currently considered enhancements.

C. Other Key Reports

1. 1999 DOT Assessment of the U.S. Marine Transportation System

Pursuant to the "Coast Guard Authorization Act of 1998" (P. L. 105-383), DOT and interested public and private stakeholders undertook a comprehensive review of conditions and needs in the MTS.[42] The assessment concluded that as comprehensive as the MTS was then, its ability to handle the emerging needs of tomorrow will be severely challenged, especially in the following areas:

Growing Levels of Demand: All users – commercial and military freight shipments, recreational and commercial passengers –increasingly demand waterborne transportation services.

Shifting User Requirements: The business environment in which American companies must operate has become more competitive. Ports and other MTS operators must meet increasingly stringent requirements to compete successfully for American business. In response, transportation providers are merging or entering into business alliances. They are deploying new technologies; larger and faster vessels; double-stacked trains for more efficiently transporting shipments over land; and advanced tracking systems so that businesses know where their goods are at any moment.

Infrastructure Concerns: The physical infrastructure and information systems that support the MTS must adapt to these changing needs. Key infrastructure issues include:

- *Dredging and marking the harbor channels that connect U.S. ports to the world.* Larger vessels, while more cost-efficient, require deeper waterways. Overall, the nation's future dredging requirements can be expected to grow.

- *Modernizing locks and dams to regulate water flow and facilitate commerce.* "By 2000, more than 44 percent of the inland waterway locks and dams will be at least 50-years old. Many locks are undersized for modern commercial barge movements."[43]

- *Improving marine terminal capacity and access to rail, road, and pipeline.* Seamless movement of goods across transportation modes and geographical areas is needed to minimize transportation costs borne by the American consumer.

- *Advancing computer, communications, and navigation technologies to increase the productivity, safety, and security of the MTS.* Technologies are generally grouped as "Intelligent Transportation Systems" (ITS), such as Differential Global Positioning Systems (DGPS), Vessel Traffic Services (VTS), Physical Oceanographic Real-Time Systems (PORTS) and Electronic Navigational Charts (ENCs).

---

[42] An Assessment of the U.S. Marine Transportation System, Report to Congress, U.S. Department of Transportation, September 1999.

[43] Ibid p. 7

Other Concerns:

Enhancing Coordination: There is an increasing need for comprehensive coordination, leadership, and cooperation among Federal, regional, State, and local agencies, as well as private-sector owners and operators.

Security: MTS providers must be vigilant to potential terrorist acts. The MTS must remain capable of supporting national security objectives – the projection of U.S. military forces and their sustainment depend 90 to 95 percent on sealift deployment.

Sustaining the Environment: MTS decision-making and planning must acknowledge and account for the fundamental interdependency between the MTS and the environment.

Safety: The rapid growth of trade and recreational opportunities in recent years has stretched many parts of the MTS to their limits. Human factors, ranging from the growth in personal watercraft use to inadequately trained crews, clearly contribute to MTS-related accidents.

Minimizing Conflicts Among Land Uses Along the Waterfront and Intermodal Connections:
Waterfront redevelopment revitalizes communities, but it leaves less land available for port development. Intermodal connections at ports also experience land constraints because of zoning and environmental regulations that restrict expansion, particularly in densely-populated areas.

Funding the System: Funding to create a MTS capable of meeting the increased demands of trade, passenger, and recreational use, coupled with national security, environmental stewardship, and safety requirements, is a public and private sector responsibility. Improvements in technology, better coordination, and process improvement will help, but not entirely relieve, the government and the private sector of growing resource and investment demands. In turn, this issue may give rise to the need for innovative financing mechanisms.

2. 2003 U.S. Chamber of Commerce Study on Trade and Transportation

Among the most recent and widely recognized studies is "Trade and Transportation", conducted by the National Chamber Foundation of the U.S. Chamber of Commerce. The study found that, "The U.S. port and intermodal freight transportation system is now being operated in many areas at the limits of its maximum capacity. Should any component of the system break down, more than one fourth of the national economy would be crippled. Such breakdowns have partially occurred in the past, and will most certainly occur in the future. The paradox is that the United States has significant reserve capacity in its freight transportation system; it is simply located in the wrong place to relieve the most critical choke points. The U.S. lacks a national program for freight transportation planning and development to focus critical scarce resources on the choke points as key gateways and corridors."[44]

---

[44] National Chamber Foundation, p. 3.

3. 2004 Transportation Research Board Special Report 279, The Marine Transportation System and the Federal Role, Measuring Performance, Targeting Improvement[45]

TRB Report 279 also found many of the same concerns about the MTS that were emphasized in the 1999 DOT MTS Report to Congress. The TRB stated, "The integration of the nation's transportation modes, particularly for the movement of freight, is a long-term phenomenon that may ultimately compel changes in Federal responsibilities and institutions. Short of such change, much can be done to ensure that the Federal government remains responsive to the needs of commerce and the public. The actions recommended in this report represent the first steps in ensuring that the MTS, and intermodalism in general, has a meaningful influence on Federal policies and decision-making processes."[46]

This report also states, "The Secretary of Transportation should seek a mandate from Congress for the DOT to take the Federal lead in measuring, monitoring, and assessing options to strengthen the MTS's contribution to the furthering of key national interests, including commerce, environmental protection, safety and security. While legislative authorization is imperative to sustain such an effort, DOT should assume this leadership role immediately thereby demonstrating the need to Congress."[47]

4. 2004 U.S. Commission on Ocean Policy – Preliminary Report

The Oceans Act of 2000 (Public Law 106-256), requires the U.S. Commission on Ocean Policy to establish findings and make final recommendations to the President and Congress for a coordinated and comprehensive national ocean policy. The Commission's preliminary report, released in April 2004, recognized the links to the national transportation infrastructure, and included recommendations for Congress and DOT to improve the MTS and intermodal system. In a key statement in the report on the MTS, the Commission stated, "An important step in allowing the U.S. marine transportation system to grow, while minimizing increased congestion, delays, and costs to U.S. businesses and consumers, is to improve the movement of cargo into and out of ports. Existing intermodal connections are inadequate to meet the expected increase in foreign trade and domestic commerce. The nation's transportation infrastructure is largely an agglomeration of competing transportation modes, each focusing on its own priorities. While this approach has produced an extensive infrastructure, a national strategy is needed to enhance the connections among these modes, including the nation's ports, and ensure greater overall effectiveness."[48] To address this condition, the Commission recommends that DOT develop a national freight transportation strategy to support continued growth of the nation's economy and international trade, and improve the links between the MTS and other components of the transportation infrastructure.[49]

---

[45] Transportation Research Board Special Report 279, The Marine Transportation System and the Federal Role, Measuring Performance, Targeting Improvement, 2004

[46] ibid, p.6:11
[47] ibid, p6:11
[48] Preliminary Report of the U.S. Commission on Ocean Policy, Governors' Draft, Washington, DC, April 2004, p. 152.

5. 2003 Maritime Administration, Industry Survey Series: Mainstream Container Services[50]

Twenty-one of the container operators participating in the U.S. Transatlantic and U.S. Transpacific trades responded to this MARAD survey. They were asked to rate and rank the services and infrastructure at U.S. East Coast and West Coast ports and compare them to European, Asian, and Canadian ports. While many of the questions raised the same issues that were in the Intermodal Access Report, the Marine Transportation System Infrastructure Needs Report noted above, and in this report, the mainline container services' order of priorities were different than those cited by the port authorities.

According to the respondents, the U.S. East and West Coast ports provided better rail and road access than any of their foreign counterparts. Rail and road access are not of serious concern to the mainstream container service operators in the short term. Overall efficiency of U.S. ports, the focus of this study requested by Congress, was rated as the 3rd worst factor compared to European ports, the 4th worst factor compared to Asian ports, and somewhat better than Canadian ports. However, as explained below, other issues are of greater concern to the mainstream container service operators in the short term.

Three of the questions addressed issues that are particularly important to U.S. port authorities in developing plans for the future:

1. Why do you divert cargo from U.S. ports to Canadian ports?

   Fifteen of the 21 respondents said that inland connections were the primary reason that they used Canadian ports in the U.S. container trades. The Harbor Maintenance Tax was cited as the second most important reason for diverting cargo to Canadian ports.

2. To what extent does your firm plan to increase its control of the following assets in the U.S.?

   Fifteen of the 21 respondents said that they plan to increase their control of U.S. terminal assets, but only two of those described their plans to increase control as significant. There was only modest interest in expanding control of other kinds of assets.

3. Carriers were asked to rank the service improvements that they expect to emphasize in 2004, from most to least important.

   The mainline container operators rated "vessel on-time arrival" and "cargo on-time delivery" as equally necessary service improvements. Costs-per-move and cargo tracking systems were rated 2nd and 3rd respectively. Improvements to terminal operations, truck dwell time at terminals, and inland transportation were significantly less important to the container services being ranked 9th, 10th and 12th respectively. Costs-per-move were consistently ranked the second-worst service feature when compared to European, Asian and Canadian ports.

---

[50] U.S. Maritime Administration, Industry Survey Series: Mainstream Container Services, 2003

70

This was the first survey of its kind and MARAD did not attempt to interpret the survey responses. However, when viewed in conjunction with the survey responses to the other key reports and the responses given in the DOT team port interviews for this report, it is clear that there are numerous factors that contribute to port efficiency and customer satisfaction. None of them can or should be addressed in a stand-alone manner by one entity or even one interest group. By working together on a systemic basis, stakeholders will be able to leverage their individual contribution to increase port efficiency and customer service to achieve a system that is greater than the sum of its parts.

D. Analysis of Port and Intermodal Congestion Challenges Identified in External Perspectives

Ports are critical links in the global supply chain, and they are strategically investing in new infrastructure facilities to keep that supply chain functioning and freight moving. However, the enormous projected freight growth, exacerbated now with important security requirements, promises to overwhelm private-sector or local entities' ability to keep pace with needed investment. An efficient supply chain will require Federal Government attention to new port capacity, as well as rail and truck capacity, all of which are extremely costly initiatives. Port congestion issues include:

Landside Access

Efficient transportation depends on connections between the road, rail, and water. In order to move waterborne cargo quickly to/from inland locations, trucks and railroads need to have effective access to ports. Often the weakest link in a port's logistics chain is the "last mile," where congested roadways or inadequate rail connections cause delays and raise transportation costs. With the expected growth in foreign trade, our nation's infrastructure will be challenged to accommodate this increase in freight movement in a timely manner, especially given the growing congestion caused by other commercial and passenger traffic. For example, the lack of left-hand traffic signals for trucks leaving marine terminals, or at-grade rail crossings on local streets, can tie up traffic and create freight transportation bottlenecks. MARAD commissioned a detailed Intermodal Access Survey that addressed these and other problem areas, as discussed earlier in this report.

Highway Access

The trucking industry is the backbone of the domestic distribution system. The most acute intermodal problem for intermodal truckers is the so-called "last mile." The last mile in or out of high volume terminals is a landside port access issue not yet fully appreciated in the freight transportation planning community.

ISTEA specifically cited the problem of inadequate intermodal connectors, and a lack of an investment program to remedy these connectors. The National Highway System (NHS) Intermodal Freight Connectors Report documents that 1,222 miles of connector roads are in far worse condition and receive less funding than other NHS routes.[51] A focused approach to improving these intermodal connectors is needed, and such a program is included in the SAFETEA legislative proposal.

---

[51] NHS Intermodal Freight Connectors, A Report to Congress, prepared by the U.S. Department of Transportation July 2000, Table 8, p. 26

Rail Access

Intermodal rail has been the fastest growing segment of traffic for the U.S. railroad industry over the past decade. U.S. rail intermodal has grown from 3.1 million units (trailers and containers) in 1980 to nearly 9 million units in 2001. Intermodal rail operations now account for about 20 percent of the revenue for the major railroads. Half of that intermodal traffic is international. Today, rail intermodal moves are highly dependent upon efficient seaports where rail traffic can move seamlessly from the ship to the rail car. This requires huge capital investments, careful planning, adequate land in and near the port, and complex institutional arrangements that must be forged to manage such projects – the achievement of which is increasingly difficult as port cities themselves expand, competing for a finite amount of space, driving up the cost of land, and generating local opposition for, by example, environmental reasons. The Southern California Alameda Corridor has been a large success. While the Alameda Corridor is a proud national achievement of improved rail access, there is a need for similar intermodal corridor projects in other heavily congested areas.

Waterside Access

Most U.S. ports are not naturally deep harbors, and unless ports are dredged, goods cannot move in the quickest, most cost-effective way through the marine transportation portion of the intermodal chain. Without unobstructed navigation channels, deep-draft ships cannot travel safely into ports. Dredging keeps ports open, safe, and competitive. However, there are challenges with respect to funding and environmental issues that affect the ports' ability to achieve necessary dredging.

Today, modern containerships are likely to need drafts of more than 45 feet. Bulk vessels may need drafts of 60 feet or more. Most ports require removal of sediment to deepen Federal access channels, provide turning basins for ships and adequate water depth alongside land-based facilities. To maintain navigable waterways, each year approximately 400 million cubic yards of material are dredged from harbors, enough to build a four-lane highway four feet deep between New York and Los Angeles. Ports must be dredged if the United States is to continue to be competitive in international trade, and this must be done in an environmentally responsible manner.

Financing Improvements

In order to keep up with changing vessel sizes and trends in world trade, ports continually update their facilities. U.S. public deep-draft ports have made sizeable advances in modernizing and expanding terminal facilities. Since 1946, ports have invested more than $25 billion, with over $1.6 billion invested in 2002 alone. Since 9/11, some of the investment dollars that would normally go into modernizing facilities for more productive and expanded intermodal transportation capacity are being diverted to fund important and necessary new port security requirements. This comes at the same time MARAD estimates that the 51 largest U.S. public ports alone have cumulative capital improvement needs (for ports, their landside intermodal connectors, and security) of approximately $35 billion over the next 10 years.[52]

---

[52] U.S. Public Ports Development Expenditure Report, U.S. Department of Transportation, Office of Ports and Domestic Shipping, May 2004.

www.ingramcontent.com/pod-product-compliance
Lightning Source LLC
Chambersburg PA
CBHW052007280526
45793CB00005B/887